The Author.   Photograph by
Mary Sealey. Exmouth.

A DOG WITH TWO TAILS.

Published by: Crystal Elizabeth Nicholson 4.10.97

© Copyright Crystal Elizabeth Nicholson 1997

ISBN 0 9531715 0 7

Reprinted 1998

Printed by: Antony Rowe Limited
                Chippenham
                Wiltshire SN14 6LH

A DOG WITH TWO TAILS.

By: Crystal Elizabeth Nicholson.

Dedicated to George Williams
Without whose diaries this book
could not have been written.

And of course, JACK. Who accompanied George on this walk. A grateful and loving friend.

'Dileas' Ever Faithful.

FOREWORD

Dear Reader,

My name is Jack and I am a black and white Collie Dog. I am the first dog to have walked around the coastline of Gt. Britain, and my master, George Williams, is the fourth man, so we have gone into the Guiness Book of Records. It was nearly 7,000 miles so I can tell you from experience it was a long, long, walk.

I was very tired when we finished and I slept for a whole week. George (my master) and I enjoyed every minute, more or less. We made a lot of money for the R.S.P.C.A. on the way and now this book is finished we are giving (after expenses), any profit from sales to the St. John Ambulance Ophthalmic Hospital.

I tell you of the time I got lost, of waking one morning to find a fox sharing our tent. Of straying onto an airforce practice area, with guns and bombs raining down on us. Our meeting up with a very merry ferryboat man in Scotland, of telling a classroom of schoolchildren about our escapade in Wales, and many more tales. Perhaps I will go into the Guiness Book of Records, as the first dog to have written a book.??

Love, Jack.

P.S. Yes, we did stop for lots of cups of tea on the way. You see, George, my master, not having a small stove, lived on cold food and water for the whole of this trip. Therefore if a cup of tea was offered, or if we passed a tea shop, he just couldn't resist a hot drink of some kind. I know you will understand.

INDEX

Chapter 1.	The seventh day.	page	5.
Chapter 2.	A Home at last.	page	8.
Chapter 3.	Seaton to Bognor Regis.	page	13.
Chapter 4.	Bognor Regis to Romford.	page	19.
Chapter 5.	Romford to Southwold.	page	25.
Chapter 6.	Southwold to Skegness.	page	30.
Chapter 7.	Skegness to Hull.	page	41.
Chapter 8.	Hull to St. Andrews.	page	48.
Chapter 9.	St. Andrews to Bonar Br.	page	58.
Chapter 10.	Bonar Bridge to Wick.	page	66.
Chapter 11.	Wick to Cape Wrath.	page	77.
Chapter 12.	Cape Wrath to Shieldaig.	page	84.
Chapter 13.	Shieldaig to Inveraray.	page	93.
Chapter 14.	Inveraray to Ayr.	page	100.
Chapter 15.	Ayr to Gretna Green.	page	108.
Chapter 16.	Gretna Green to M/combe.	page	119.
Chapter 17.	Morecombe to Anglesey.	page	126.
Chapter 18.	Anglesey to Fishguard.	page	138.
Chapter 19.	Fishguard to Swansea.	page	145.
Chapter 20.	Swansea to Dunster.	page	152.
Chapter 21.	Dunster to Newquay.	page	162.
Chapter 22.	Newquay to Falmouth.	page	169.
Chapter 23.	Falmouth to Exminster.	page	179.
Chapter 24.	Homeward Bound.	page	188.

CHAPTER 1

THE SEVENTH DAY

Jack gazed out of his pen with a dejected air. It was the seventh day, everyone knew what the seventh day meant. Tom the big mastiff in the next pen told him. It meant that the local Vet would soon be arriving to take away all the unloved dogs that nobody wanted. It was their last day in Police custody, there was however the R.S.P.C.A. lady, but she didn't always have a lot of room.

Jack remembered how he'd been thrown out of the car on Dartmoor. He was always talking and interfering with peoples conversation. The last words he heard were "If that dog doesn't stop making that ** noise, he'll be chucked out." And that is exactly what happened. Jack was only saying what a nice ride it was.

He had gazed around forlornly after the car had gone. A sheep, munching grass nearby gave him a mournful look. Jack didn't know which way to start walking. He decided as night had nearly come to look for a place to sleep. He found a shallow hole in a grassy bank and settled down.

He woke up stiff in the morning. The heavy dew had settled on his fur and made him very uncomfortable, he drank a little water from a nearby stream but he was so hungry.

He trotted out to the nearby road and decided he must find some houses where someone might be kind enough to give him a bone. He walked for hours and hours and saw nothing. Presently a car drew up near him, and he heard a low whistle. Quickly turning he saw a young man get out of the car, he called to Jack, "Are you lost boy," Jack trotted over obediently and got a pat on the head. The young man coaxed him into the car, Jack thought he must not say anything that is how he got chucked out last time. He kept his head low as the car picked up speed. We'll see what we can do at the station he said.

Arriving at the Police H.Q. he went inside and then came back. We have just one pen left he said to Jack. this is your lucky day. He led Jack to the back yard where eight pens were built. Each had a box with a warm blanket and a bowl of water. Jack was thankful just to climb into the box and fall asleep. A rattle of his pen door announced the arrival of food, but Jack was fast asleep, tomorrow would have to do.

Jack soon got friendly with the other dogs. Tom lived next door, but he was very old, he said he'd had enough, he'd been badly treated all his life until a kindly policeman had rescued him. He was happy here, but really he was prepared to go to his dog heaven or wherever dogs went.

Fluffy lived the other side, she'd only been in kennels for two days and had run away from her mistress which she was now sorry about. She was an overstuffed pekinese and thoroughly spoilt.

Tom told him that the dogs were only kept for seven days and then unless the R.S.P.C.A. lady came they had to be put down if no one wanted them. He and two other dogs further down the yard and Jack were on their seventh day.

Suddenly, a door opened, and a lady policeman (as Jack knew her) came out with an older lady. "There is Fluffy" the old lady said. Fluffy jumped up and down with delight. She promised in her doggy way that she wouldn't run away again. The two of them went home so happy and Jack wondered if anyone would come for him.

The day wore on, the dogs were all getting a bit agitated now except for Tom, who was glad to just lay down in a bit of comfort. Suddenly the whispers went up and down the line. The lady from the R.S.P.C.A. is here. Up shot the heads of every dog as the door opened once again. Up and down the line the lady went. I have only three pens available she said and you have seven dogs here. Some of the dogs had a few more days to go before their time was up, someone might claim them. She looked at Tom longingly but said he was too old for a new home as much as she would like to help, and the cuts on his back would still need attention from the vet. Tom didn't really mind, as he'd said to Jack he'd had enough. Jack however was lucky, he and two other nondescript types from the other end were taken to a small van and put in. Papers were exchanged and they were off. The lady had gone a couple of miles when she suddenly turned the van around and went back, she had obviously forgotten something. After waiting outside for a few minutes the back door of the van was opened and Tom was lifted in. I just couldn't leave you the lady said, but goodness knows where I can put you. All the other dogs called out in chorus he can share my pen, but Jack just curled up next to Tom, happy to see his friend again.

CHAPTER 2
A HOME AT LAST

George walked up and down the pens at The Sidmouth Animal Rescue park (A.R.C. for short). I spoke as he went past. "Yes, I think you and I will get on very well" he said to me. A lady came and unclipped the gate and I was free. I tried in my doggy way to tell George how much I appreciated this, and I think he understood.

George had been looking for a certain type of dog for a long time. He was now sure he had found his companion and he could at last put into action the promise he had made when he left his full time service in the R.A.F. in 1979.

For the last three years he had been planning the 'Round Britain walk' and now he had a firm walking companion (One that wouldn't let him down) by the name of Jack, a border collie, who had picked out George as his new master before George had decided on him.

It was day one and at 12 noon on the 1st of March 1983 we, George, and I intend to start our walk around the coastline of Britain. (Asked if I would like to go I replied YES) so we are ready for off, we have had quite a bit of publicity including an article in a magazine entitled 'THE GREAT OUTDOORS' who informed us that if we succeed in this venture, George will be the 4th man and I will be the first dog to walk the coastline of this Island.

Other publicity includes two reports in the local paper and two interviews on the local radio. At our start from Topsham in Devon the Express and Echo photographer was there, and friends and neighbours

Printed by Express and Echo Exeter.
'Goodbye Kisses.'

Printed by Exmouth Herald.
'One man and his dog.'

from nearby who had erected a 'Good Luck' sign on a lamp post. George and I were ready, and over 7,000 miles lay before us. We took a last look at home and set off over the Topsham Marshes.

We were going to walk down the railway lines to Exmouth, but this plan had to be shelved as THE WESTERN MORNING NEWS had phoned to say they would meet us on route, so it had to be the main road. The Western Morning news man was very nice and took several pictures of us near The Nutwell Court and then George and I were on our way again to Exmouth. We arrived eventually at the offices of the Exmouth Herald and had a pleasant reception, but I would have loved a bowl of water. More photographs and then straight through Exmouth down to the sea front. I find out to my disgust that I can't drink sea water but I soon enjoyed the open space of the sea shore. I ran up and down and rolled in the soft sand and really spoiled myself. We reached the end of the sea front and then up over the cliff to encounter the first part of the coastal path that would take us, hopefully around the edge of our beautiful island.

I came across a field full of sheep, which were in full view of me through a wire fence. Stupid things they were, just following one another. I just carried on walking and completely ignored them. George had worried about this quite a lot I know, before we started as I am supposed to be a Sheepdog, but he feels a lot more relaxed now knowing that I had no interest in chasing them.

We eventually arrived at Budleigh and helped a lady catch 'Henry' her little dachshund who had made a quick break for it. With a bit of luck I was able to corner 'Henry' and George then handed him back to his owner. After this good deed we went into the town where George purchased two oranges amd a bar of chocolate and one pound of apples, which we seemed to have eaten quite quickly.

George and I set off up the river Otter to find a place to set up our first camp. The time was 6.15pm, it took us half an hour to get sorted out, as both of us were tired out we couldn't eat our tea, but will have it for breakfast tomorrow morning. In fact I dropped off to sleep in the long grass, and when the tent was up I had to be carried inside. George thankfully climbed into his sleeping bag and soon we were both out for the count.

Day 2. We awoke at 9.30 after a restless night. George has not yet quite got the hang of his sleeping bag or of putting the tent up.I woke up to find that we were trying to sleep on the same bit of grass and were cuddled up together. On later inspection we found that we had put the tent up on a gentle slope, so our apparent passion for each other was caused by the force of gravity.

George took the tent down in the rain while listening to his small radio, which was lodged in a nearby tree. We ate our dinner from the previous night for breakfast,and then we were off again to continue our journey.

The mist was on the cliff tops which obstructed our view of the sea, but we could hear the waves on the beach below. As we stepped onwards towards Sidmouth I found half a dead rabbit and made as much a meal of it as time would allow before George was almost out of sight and I had to call to him. On through Otterton and Newton Poppleford before finding the coastal path again. On arrival at Sidmouth went to the Post office and purchased cards and stamps to start the card campaign to inform the family of our progress, and then on to The Sidmouth Herald where they seemed to be expecting us. We started to make our way to Newton Poppleford where George's friend, Steve Phillips lived, there we had been promised a bath and a bed for the night. We were made very welcome with a soft chair and a comfy bed. I wasn't allowed this luxury at home, but no-one had the heart to turn me out of the chair and when a cushion was offered to me to sleep on, I didn't want to refuse. George had a few beers with Steve and then had a 'nice bath' and slept in a comfy bed also. I was really tired and failed to make it to the garden and disgraced myself on the mat inside the door. No fuss was made and both George and I had a wonderful nights sleep.

In the morning with most of our aches and pains soothed away, we headed for The Blue Ball at Sidford, where we had arranged to meet Mrs Shrimpton and some members of the A.R.C. We arrived safely and one lady had informed me that she had sponsored me for one penny per mile of the 7,000 miles involved in this venture. Two ladies doing 'Meals on wheels' donated a handful of coppers which George passed over to Mrs Shrimpton, and looking around me I was very pleased with the number of people who had turned out to wish us well. Mum (who had driven from Exmouth), of course was there and our old friend The Rev. Gerry Moore. I noticed several notes being handed to Mrs Shrimpton by well wishing supporters of A.R.C. After much greeting and hand-shaking and a drink of beer, the men from the B.B.C. at Plymouth arrived. They suggested we do a filming session, so George and I obliged, however as the night was now well spent we decided, that one more night at Steves Cottage would not be amiss. In the morning with good wishes we were sent on our way. George and I went over the bridge to tackle Salcombe Hill. It was raining and he donned his wet weather gear and I just shook myself occasionally as we climbed upwards and onwards. George looked around at one stage and found out I was not following as I had

met another friend of my own class. After many
whistles and yells I decided I had better leave my new
found friend who said he was a stray and make tracks
after George. Once again, together, we tackled the
remaining hill.

The rain had made the pathway very slippery and his
R.A.F. boots didn't always grip fully,tep by step he
eventually got to the top, or at least he arrived to
where I was sitting waiting for him with a dog type
grin if its possible for a dog to grin. After a last
look at Sidmouth George and I were over a stile and
once more going along a footpath.

We arrive in Beer.we didn't stop as we wanted to make
contact with the A.R.C. supporters, the Coopers of
Vernon Cafe in Harbour Rd., Seaton. We pressed on
through Beer on our way,towards Seaton.

We meet up with a lady out walking her dog,I wanted to
play, but the other little dog was not interested.
This lady ran a shop in Seaton called 'The Golden
Hamper' which sold lots of interesting food. She gave
us a packet of dog biscuits and a tin of dog meat on
the house for me, and to George she gave six currant
buns and then following her directions we went on our
way to find Vernon cafe, this didn't take long. We
received a great welcome and George was quickly given
four cups of tea and a nice meal. I was given more
biscuits and a pint of milk, After this we found the
coastal path again which took us over a golf course
where we temporarily lost the footpath. It was
getting dark now, so we looked for a place to camp.
George and I have found a barn full of hay, I have
just been sick and brought up all the milk, never mind
we at least have shelter as its just started to rain
again. Time to close down its 7.15pm. We are both
soon fast asleep.

CHAPTER 3
From Seaton to Bognor Regis

I was awakened at 8.30 by a banging sound On investigating I found it was a couple of seagulls making a noise with their beaks on the roof, I soon chased them off.

As George was still asleep I thought I would have a nose around myself. There was a lovely big cow pat on the path, it looked quite new as it was steaming. I went gingerly over and took a sniff and then had a good roll. I wriggled about, and then I got up and rolled over the other side and even got some in my hair, it was lovely. George however had woken up by this time, and he was cross. I couldn't understand why, but he said I stank. He took me down to the sea and gave me a good wash off. It was jolly cold that time of the morning, but it didn't make any difference.George was muttering all kinds of things, I didn't understand any of the words, which I had never heard before. Anyway we soon got under way with George still muttering.

We see Lyme Regis in the distance, we meet up with the Town Crier who takes us to The Volunteer Inn where George is given a pint and a bowl of soup, and I was given a bowl of water by the landlady who was also the Mayoress of Lyme Regis. We are both treated like royalty. Apparently George and I were on Telly last night, I would have liked to have seen that, but we decided to leave the Telly at home

We arrived in Charmouth, there is a wooden bridge to cross which I didn't like the look of so I swam the river. George said it would do me good as I still stank.George was carrying a bone (given to me by the

butcher in Lyme Regis), which he gave to me when we
stopped for a break and it was really nice. We
settled into our tent about 7 pm.

Next day, we set off towards Bridport and then West
Bay. George had bought a tin of soup and one of beans
to keep us going while we walked along Chesil Beach.
We have been told it is 17 miles long. The Spring
tide was well out which was lucky for us as it left a
hard footpath of sand to walk on, much better than the
pebbles. George and I have found an old war-time pill
box to sleep in. It was a bit smelly, but then so am
I George said, so we made an early night of it.

Day 7, we weren't very comfortable last night so we
are up early to-day. The sun is shining, and after we
have both had a paddle in the sea we are off. We
arrive at Portland Bill at 1 pm. We both rested for
an hour and had some food. On we went all afternoon
until early evening, when we decided to stop.

Seeing a barn in the not so distant field we made our
way over to it and were soon asleep. However as the
mist came down we were awakened every thirty seconds
by a loud wail from the lighthouse, announcing to all
and sundry to be aware of the danger of the rocks. We
eventually fell asleep from exhaustion. We awoke at
4.15 am. and decide we have had enough. We get up,
pack our things and once more we are on the road.
Hurrying away from Portland, not too impressed with
the surroundings, we head for Weymouth. Of course all
the shops are still closed, but we head for the local
newspaper office and when they open we announce our
arrival. More pictures, and a very nice newspaper man
by the name of Alistair Nisbet took down our story.
The press gave us a big teapot which George was able
to get six cups of tea out of, and I had a bowl of
milk. Then we walked the length of the seafront, up
over the hill and past Pontins Camp, when another

gentleman of the press caught us up and wanted more photographs. We obliged happily when a dog biscuit was offered. We now headed towards Lulworth Cove and hope to reach there by 5 pm. We had a little rest on the way, and I managed a little 'kip' in the long grass. This is a wonderful life!!

Day 10. We awoke at 3.30 am. So cold, that we decided to get up to try and get the circulation moving. It was still dark but I found a heap of chucked out chips from someone, I decided to have breakfast early and soon gobbled them up.

We set off towards Lymington as the sun was rising, looks as though it might be a nice day. We bought some apples and oranges in a little shop as we were passing through a village, George is particularly fond of fruit, but I myself could take it or leave it. The lady in the shop was quite excited when she saw us and gave us her daily newspaper. There on the front page was a picture of George and me, and our story. We were stars at last. Onward we went again with nothing of great interest all day. After a few miles on a bit of a main road a footpath looms up. I was so pleased, I don't like being on a lead. We stopped in a small copse and George and I had a raw egg each, and another bone which was given to me by the last lady. This would be a rather nice place to camp for the night so George put the tent up. We turn in at 6.45pm.

It was a very pretty spot where we stopped, all full of snowdrops. A hint of Spring well on its way. We arrived in Lymington where George did his Postcard bit, by sending off a card to say how far we have reached to Mum and sister-in-law Sue. . Also one to Gerry Moore to let him know we are getting near and to get the bath water ready. George said I certainly need one after rolling in that muck.

We passed through the countryside in Hampshire, including the park at Beaulieu. Here I met a lady who gave me a tin of cat food -- I suppose it will do in an emergency, but I'm not too sure, will have to see how desperate I am. We met a young cyclist who was on his way to Hythe, where we hoped to catch the ferry the next morning. He walked quite a way with us. When we got to Hythe we found the ferry but decide to stay this side of the river until tomorrow morning. The day was getting on and we still had a meal to eat and erect our tent. We phoned home and George had a natter with Mum, I think he finds the last hour before making camp drags a bit, and it was nice to hear a friendly voice. I wuff-wuff into the phone and then Mum sent me a big kiss. Settling down that night George bathed his feet in the river. He had quite a lot of blisters, they looked very painful but he said he's O.K. I try to help him by licking them, but George didn't approve.

He should have four legs like me and then they would only get half as tired. George and I had a quick look at the boats going up and down Southampton water before settling down for the night, which was reasonably restful.

Next morning we pack our kit and make our way to the ferry. I was certainly not very happy when I saw the amount of water we had to cover before we reached the other side. In fact I didn't want to go on the ferry at all. I kicked up such a fuss that George had to carry me on. I felt so embarrassed I lay on the floor for the whole crossing and kept mumbling to myself, and was very pleased when the whole thing was over. I couldn't get off fast enough.

We find the newspaper office for our report of progress, lots more photos and then with a shake of hands we are again on our way. However there was a bonus as we were on our way to Gerry and Erica's house at Gosport. (Friends of George). The lead was put on me again as we are travelling over all sorts of different roads. We passed a signpost which read 'Gosport 6 miles' we did not mind as we knew a welcome would await us there. We eventually arrived at No.13. Gerry's Mum was there and I had a lovely bowl of clean water and George had a nice cup of tea. George and I are at home. Later when Erica and Gerry came home we go to a friends house and saw a recording from all the coverage that the B.B.C. had done of us. I didn't think a lot of it, but George thought it was marvellous, and wanted to see it run through again.

After two pints of beer for George we decided to call it a day especially as it was then 11 pm. I was given a nice warm bed in the kitchen, and George had a real bed to sleep in. We are both soon fast asleep.

To-day is Sunday, Gerry's big day of the week. When he and Erica went off for their first service I was given a good bath in a tin tub in the yard. After I was made presentable we took Gerry's two boys, Joel and Ben for a short walk just to limber up, we then had a fantastic lunch of which I had the bones, all nice and warm and juicy. We finished off with a lovely restful afternoon and then went to meet the family from Sunday service. This again was enjoyed as we had tea and cakes afterwards at the church, and I went around to everyone for little tit-bits and lots of petting, even a saucer of tea. Home again and bed at Gerry's house, very, very acceptable.

Day 14. Awoke at 7.30 by the action in the household. The boys are getting ready for school. Radio Solent had sent out a lady reporter to take our story also a reporter from a Portsmouth paper. We feel quite important. We must get on our way again soon, before we become too comfortable. Gerry drives us to the ferry so that we could continue with our walk at the point where we diverted ourselves a few days ago. We head towards Hayling Island. Then there was another short ferry ride. I personally think the ferries are really unsafe. George has to carry me again, so I shut my eyes tight and pretended I was in a lovely wood with trees around. Arriving safely on the other side we were asked if we were the chaps from Devon who were walking around the world!! I was very pleased that George corrected him by saying we are only walking around Great Britain, and the islands, nearly 7000 miles, and enough for a starter I think.

Through Chichester and on towards Bognor Regis to look for a place to sleep. We eventually found an old farm cart, with just enough room for the two of us to crawl under. By then it was 6.25 pm and getting cold. We were just 4½ miles from Bognor, and George says he feels happy with our progress.

CHAPTER 4

Bognor Regis to Romford

The traffic near our farm cart is very noisy. We set off for Bognor and arrive at 9.30 at the newspaper offices. After our duties for the day we head for Littlehampton along the front. We stop for a bite to eat at a little transport cafe. Very good value. I even had a special plate with some scraps in. Arriving at Worthing we pass a cottage where two ladies call us inside and give George a cup of tea. They made a great fuss of me and they told us they had been watching our progress on the news. They raided their larder and I had two tins of dog meat given to me. They said they still had one left for their dog, and then they could do some more shopping. A good rest and then its off to Brighton, finding a little hole to sleep in on the way. Report to the newspaper offices where we both receive a smashing welcome with countless cups of tea and biscuits for me. On towards Newhaven by the Undercliff walk, where I can run free. Stopping for egg and chips. One and a half portions.

In the morning George inspects his big toe which is troubling him. It is so badly swollen he has decided to leave his boots behind and start on his Clark's shoes. A little premature but walking is difficult.

I try to help him as much as I can, but I'm really not big enough to give him a lift on my back. George is limping a lot and I am worried. We stop to bathe his toe in a little clear stream, and I help by giving his toe a lick which is not appreciated by George. He should know better than to push me away, anyone knows a dog can heal its own wounds by licking. We now have to tackle the Seven Sisters Cliffs. The thick mist

comes down and I have a job finding George so I decide
to stay close. Arriving in Eastbourne we report
into the Newspaper office and then find a nice kind
butcher who offered me two bones, lovely. He wrapped
them up in newspaper and I carried them to our next
stop-over with my mouth drooling all of the time.
George buys some fish and chips with an extra piece of
fish for me, we sit on the end of the pier and eat our
supper, plus one bone for me. I really am full up and
make a huge bulking noise, George says "Pardon" for
me, but I feel very full and happy.

Apparently we are waiting here for Andrew to pick us
up and take us home with him for the night. That will
be nice, we really are getting spoilt. I hope George
has friends all around the edge of G.B. but somehow I
doubt it. We sleep in a civilized manner and have a
wonderful meal. I could have stayed a bit longer, but
George says we must head for Bexhill. Next day we
are dropped off at our picking up point. George
learnt from some fishermen that we could stay on the
beach, tide permitting, until we reached Hastings. I
had a good roll and ran around in circles chasing my
tail, no trouble with my toes.

We walk into the town a bit and find a large expanse
of grass outside of a Health Authority building. It
looks ideal, so after asking the advice from a
friendly local 'bobby.' we erect our tent for the
night, behind some bushes, (where it was stated he
couldn't see us), as it is now quite dark. I chase a
town cat who was sniffing around and then I woke
George up at 1 am as a fox had joined us in our tent.
George told me to get off his feet as I was too heavy.
As I was near his nose I gave him a friendly lick.
Realizing that I couldn't be six foot long, he shone
his torch at his feet, and two bright green eyes shone
back. George threw his boot at the fox who had

settled down for the night, and then I had to retrieve
it. This happened in the middle of a busy town.

First thing in the morning we were on our way before
anyone found our campsite. Heading for Rye. George
chats for a while to a workman who is measuring the
road. George and I help him with his tape measure,
and then as he wished us Good luck we go on our way
again. It is my turn to have a sore toe, George is
concerned but I find some soft grass to walk on. We
will look for a doggy doctor in Rye, George says.

We find a spot to kip down for the night but it is
bitterly cold, I cuddle into George as much as
possible. The next day we wake up to the rain, George
dresses up in his wet gear and we soon cross the
border into Kent. We head for New Romney, it could be
the Romney Marshes we are crossing, everything looks
so bleak and wet, not to mention the wind. It is late
in the afternoon when we find an old deserted house
with a large porch, big enough for George and I for
the night. We have a good feed, we are sheltered from
the rain so we have a good nights sleep. George
writes up his diary first, with a lot of grunts, we
snuggle into together and are soon dead to the world.
We wake up next morning to a watery sun and are soon
on our way. We meet some people who confirm that we
are on the Romney Marshes. George tells me all the
stories of Dr. Syn and smugglers etc:- We can now add
that Jack and his master George Williams slept there.
We hope to reach Folkstone to-day so we must not hang
about.

Leaving Romney we head for Hythe. We arrive early and
George looks for a cafe for a cup of tea, but nothing
is open yet. It is a lovely wide seafront, and I
manage to leave my mark on the pavement edge, George
is cross and says 'use the gutter' but I was in a bit
of a hurry. We find the newspaper office where we met

two nice ladies who told us to head for the main
newspaper office in Folkestone. I did however get a
biscuit, and George a cup of tea. It was afternoon
before we set out for Folkestone after our extended
mid morning break and all the fuss, we find the office
in Folkestone as directed and have a wonderful
reception. We are told that another chap, called
Bowles, was here earlier. He is also walking the
coastline with a dog, so I won't be the first dog
after all, never mind, a lot can happen over 7000
miles.

I get on really well with the Editor and he even
offers me a home if I would like to stay, but George
is my master and he rescued me from a certain death so
I decide to stay with him. I thank the Editor and we
are soon on our way again, after more cups of tea and
biscuits. At 6 p.m. we find an old war time Pill Box.
We decide that this will do nicely for the night.

The sea is rough and the wind is blowing cold. I put
my nose inside the building, find a warm corner and
I'm soon fast asleep. Awoke at 6.30 am, George gave
me breakfast, looked outside the Pill Box and saw rain
and mist. It's wet weather gear to-day.

We make our way along the cliff tops. We have to
skirt around several army firing ranges. I feel a bit
frisky and chase my tail, the mist is still with us,
but I see a barbed wire fence in front of me which I
decide I can easily jump. Wrong decision. The wire
scapes across my tummy, and grips me tight. I hang in
a very undignified fashion upside down. My yelps of
pain soon bring George running. He carefully lifts my
back legs clear of the wire and examines my tummy, he
says there is no real damage, so once again we
continue our walk. I stay close this time, as we
continue and wait for the little swing gates to be

opened for me and walk through in a dignified manner. We make good progress to Deal.

A force 8 gale accompanies us across a golf course and we decide to try and find a sheltered spot to camp the night. It's getting dark and a nice deep sand bunker is as good a place as any. We get good shelter and we will be away early in the morning. George erects the tent after a struggle with the wind, and we are soon both asleep.

Next day we are up bright and early and soon we arrive at Westgate-on-sea. We have now completed the South Coast until we reach Cornwall at the end of our walk. We try to rest in a seaside shelter. We are very cold, but we watch a beautiful sunset and all is well. On again the next day towards Herne Bay, passing the Reculver towers (bouncing bomb waters), and then met up with a Mr. Watson and his dog Bess. We are invited back to his house for a meal and a cup of tea. I am having a bit of trouble eating. George looks in my mouth and finds a twig wedged across the roof of my mouth. He removes this, much to my relief, and mops out the blood of which there is quite a fair amount. After a nice drink of clean water all is well.

Setting out once more and getting a few miles behind us we hear a car, Mr and Mrs Watson have followed us in their car and brought us a hot steak and kidney pie each. Lovely, I soon gobble mine down and look for more, but there is nothing doing. We say good-bye once again and set our faces towards the next town which will be Whitstable. We pass a long shingle beach called 'The Street' which stretched out into the bay, most unusual formation. It's to do with the tides we are told. I found a huge pile of food, cooked meats etc:- and really gorged myself. I was sorry afterwards as I had diarrhoea and sickness. George says thats what happens when you are greedy.

Whitstable newspaper office takes pictures and hears our story. I am worn out from my eating orgy and crash out on the floor and have a sleep. We were offered a nice bed for the night, one of our planned stopping places with a Mrs Brant. We have fish and chips, a nice hot bath and a good warm bed on a very cold night. George phones home to tell of our progress. All is well, except George has a bit of a pain in his shin. My pains have all gone for the moment. The clocks go forward to-morrow so we are fed and ready for off about 9 am. in the morning.

Printed by Portsmouth and Sunderland Newspapers Ltd., 'The Editor liked me.'

CHAPTER 5.

Romford to Southwold.

We have been walking for 38 days to-day. Southend is 26 miles away. Some children are waiting for George along the way and want his autograph, one little lad dipped my paw in some mud and pressed it into his book. The others said it looked a mess but I myself thought it was quite good. We all wave goodbye and get under way again.

The next day we are awoken at 5.15 am by heavy rain beating down on our tent. We are nice and dry, perhaps it will have stopped by the time we are ready to go. We find a signpost which says 15 miles to Southend, so we plod on with a quick cup of tea at a Mobile van, for George, and a large hot sausage for me. It was so hot I had to wait for a while for it to cool. We eventually arrive at Southend to find Radio Essex is still another 3 miles on. When we do arrive it was full of school kids who were very interested in me. However I just couldn't keep my eyes open and was soon fast asleep on the floor. George did a short interview he told me, but no-one could wake me up for a wuff-wuff. We will listen to the radio to-morrow morning. We go to the sea front to ring up Jack Watson, brother of Neil at Herne Bay. We are invited for a hot meal with masses of hot tea, and we can use his garden shed for the night. We get up the next morning, we have porridge and toast and listen to the radio, and then once more on the road to Rochford. The sun is shining and the weather is good. After we find the ferry isn't running to cross the river Crouch, we have to take a long detour for Malden. We decide to call it a day and look for a place to sleep for the night. George erects the tent by a stream and then washes his socks. I'm quite pleased about this

as they had begun to pong a bit. He then sits on the
bank and soaks his feet in the stream, I bet all the
fish keep out of the way. After drying his feet
George writes up his diaries. We have a good supper
and turn in early for a nice quiet sleep.

A little while later, at 7.30p.m. we are awakened by a
gentleman who has stopped his car to inform us that
where we are camped is a tidal area for the river, and
it is now rising. We quickly move our gear to a more
sociable place and settle down once more. We pack our
kit in the rain the next morning and set off for
Malden, which is ten miles away. The sun starts to
shine as we near Malden, we stop by the Police station
to eat our lunch and to catch up on notes. George
meets up with a chap who has a dog called Lucy. We
get on well together, pity we are both on leads. This
man tells George that he is on a crusade. He wants
all the world to talk the same language. He shows
George strange maps of his plans for world government,
and how he wants lots of tunnels under all the seas,
and a vast railway system. He then says he is a
Democratic Communist and will support Mr Foot. As we
try to edge away he tells George that he has been in
the local Looney Bin as his family thought he was mad.
His dog seemed sane enough and she told me so. George
called to him to keep up the good work and we made our
escape. I felt a bit sorry for him, he seemed glad to
have someone to talk to. The last we saw of him he
was posting letters to the American President, our
Prime Minister, the Pope and many more eminent people.

George and I head for Colchester, a little way on a
nice lady called to us and wanted to know if we were
the walkers around Britain. George said we were. She
walked with us quite a way with her dog who had the
longest nose on a dog I have ever seen. She bred and
entered dogs in exhibitions all over the country. She
looked at me and said I was in excellent condition.

She didn't ask my pedigree, which was just as well.
We say goodbye and carry on our way passing through
Tiptree, Colchester is just 9 miles away. On our way
we spot a forest, then the improbable looms up, we
also spot a shed. Goodness knows why it is here.
Nicely constructed of timber, we decide to spend the
night. I get through the doorway and fall straight
asleep. I will eat my supper for breakfast.

Day 42. I wake at 7 am. after a wonderful nights
sleep. I see a cock pheasant in the forest. I nearly
had a tasty breakfast, but the thing spread its wings
and flew away. Pity I can't fly too.

We report to the newspaper offices and get pictures
and stories. We move onto the Clacton road. My foot
is hurting and I tell George so, he has a good look
and then pulls out a big thorn. I yelp, and then say I
am sorry by giving his nose a good lick. George says
thats what happens when I chase off on my own.

A signpost says Clacton 3½ miles, we also see a very
wet field with a load of sheds. We investigate a
little closer and find that one of them would be
ideal. We make ourselves comfortable for the night,
and although its early, just gone past 5 pm., we
decide to call it a day, and hope for brighter weather
tomorrow.

Awake to several sounds in the night, I poked my nose
outside the tent at one time and it was snowing. I
quickly crept inside again. On the way to Clacton the
next morning the snow turns to rain, but it's bitterly
cold. We're told that we can get to Fremington-on-
Sea by staying on the beach. This is good news as I
like to run free and do a bit of digging.

Near Frinton-on-Sea a man asks if we are the folk
walking around the edge. We say "Yes", he says that

he's from Anglia T.V. and asks for our story. We spend about 1½ hrs being filmed and then say Cheerio!

On further we have the offer of a warm bed and a meal which we cannot refuse. We watch our T.V. programme with which we are impressed, and I have a lovely bone. The next day the sun is shining as we set off for Harwich. We were so sorry to say cheerio to Jill and her family, they really made us very welcome. Lots of people come out to cheer us on our way, it seems they were all watching T.V. last night. A man in a road sweeper pulls up to wish us good luck, several cars wave to us as we go on our way, (I mean the drivers not the actual cars). Walking is easy at present as we are going along the flat Essex countryside.

We are invited by a lady passing motorist to call in to see her husband at Great Oakley Hall, close by. We eventually arrived and George knocked gingerly on the door which he thought looked like the tradesmans entrance. George and I were invited in for lunch, and I saw through the open door a great hall, beautiful furniture and masses and masses of books. George had a meal off a long dining table in the kitchen, there were lots and lots of farm dogs all laying around the kitchen floor, I wondered if I dare speak to them, but I thought they probably had blue blood and I had better keep to myself. I sat obediently by George and waited for the next move. I had a very posh bowl put by my nose, and I tried to eat my dinner very daintily. Soon it was all over, George was wished "God Speed" as we waved our good-byes.

On arrival at Felixstowe we met a kindly person who took us to the Dock area, and then stood us a cup of tea and a bowl of water. He offered us a lift in the direction we were going, I said 'Yes' but I was ignored, George said we were supposed to be walking around Britain, so walk we must. He said he understood and gave George £5 for the A.R.C. As we passed through villages on our way to Woodbridge we came across a school called Bucklesham.

All the children crowded at the railings, they had seen us on telly last night. Two teachers then arrived, we were wished well and all the children cheered us until we were out of sight.

A forest which looks inviting. George says we will spend the night here, I don't really know if he pitched the tent or just slept under the stars, I was too tired to keep awake to find out. Some time during the night I heard two snuffing noises, I barked to wake George, he shone his torch and saw two deer gazing down at us. The light frightened them and they were soon off. I slept the rest of the night with one eye open, just in case.

I woke George up by standing on him, I was not too happy about the forest, there were a lot of noises I didn't understand, it was daylight anyway, we packed our things and after breakfast we were on our way to Aldburgh, we have been going 46 days to date, it seems like an eternity. Eventually we arrive at Thorpeness.

George and I feel good, we have had a little rest and some refreshment and we were now heading for Sizewell power station and then on to Durwich.

Here in a cafe, George met about forty schoolchildren, out on a hike. After talking to them all for a while, the master bought George a huge pot of tea and a meal, and we were again set up for the next part of our journey around East Anglia. We are heading for Southwold and we can see the lighthouse with its flashing light in the distance. It's now getting to the end of the day, George is looking for a place to sleep and tomorrow we will tackle Southwold.

CHAPTER 6.

Southwold to Skegness.

After leaving the area of timber buildings we climb a hill on route to our next port of call. Here a group of people who had seen us on the T.V. were gathered, and were so interested that George had to give them a re-count of our story so far. I went around with a cap in my mouth, making a collection for the A.R.C. The T.V. photographers and news people were here too. I preened myself and sat up well. George told them how lucky he was to be healthy, he isn't suffering from anything at the moment, except a swollen head. He was able to do what he was doing, and thought often of the people who can't but would like to.

Eventually we were on our way again, with wishes of good luck, and Keep Walking!! etc. It really made our day and we set off in great spirit. George had been wondering if it was all worth it a little while ago, I know, because he was nattering to himself coming up that last hill. He always talks to himself when he is a bit miserable, I suppose I could do the same.

We pass Sizewell Power Station, quite a massive structure, there are 'Keep Out' notices everywhere. All a bit frightening to me. Men with big Alsatians were patrolling the grounds, and one came over and chatted to George. Rollo - a huge Alsatian - said he often chased off intruders, and if he could catch one, he'd tear them to bits. I imagined arms and legs flying everywhere, and told him quite distinctly that I and George had no intentions of walking on his land. He said that was O.K. then. I told him we were walking 7000 miles, and he said, "rather you than me". We said our Good-byes and continued on our way, I had nightmares of Rollo tearing George and me into little bits that night, and George had to wake me once or twice so stop me muttering.

We head down the cliff for the beach, which makes easier walking, and we pass through Durwich. George washes his socks in the sea. They will probably be a bit stiff, but at least he will get rid of the smell. He walks about a mile barefoot, nipping in and out of the waves, he enjoys having his feet free for a while, now me, I've always got my feet free, and I told George he should do this more often. George comes to a row of huts on the sand, and then a cafe. While he enjoys a cup of tea, and chatting to quite a few people, I have a race around the sand with a lot of the town's dogs. Soon the newsmen arrive and lots more people, George and I are treated to a jolly good meal, which pleases us, and then on our way again.

George posted off the money we had collected for A.R.C. when we reached Lowestoft, we try to get rid of it pretty quickly as George doesn't like to carry much money. We see several dead trees on the beach, sticking up out of the sand. We look up and realize there has been a great landslide where the waves have eroded away the cliffs. We even see the foundations of a building, all twisted up and left for lost. The shingle beach is getting harder to walk on, but its better than the road, we meet a couple along the beach collecting certain pebbles, they are from King's Lynn, they give George a few details about the Wash, but all that is ahead. George and I press on for Kessingland Chalton and Lowestoft. A man further along the beach had just caught an 8lb cod, he called to George as I passed and asked if I was the dog walking around the edge. I wuffed 'Yes' and George told him our story so far, and then admired and congratulated him on the huge fish he had just caught.

It was an absolutely beautiful day, we met two lady swimmers, who were round the year swimmers. It was too cold for George yet, he said, but I didn't mind a quick dip in and out I said. George and I walked with them to the centre of Lowestoft, where we all went into a cafe for a cup of tea. George and I had a sausage roll each, and then they said if George would give them Mum's address, they would write to her and tell her we were both O.K. and doing well.

We leave our new friends and pass the dockyard area, and a chap directs us out of Lowestoft and walks with us quite a way until we are on the beach again. George sees a long line of bunkers from the 1939 war, we inspect them and select one for our overnight stay. It is getting colder now, I don't somehow think we shall get such a nice day tomorrow. We close down, having finished our 47th. day since leaving home.

After a morning roll in the sand I trot back to the bunker to find George still asleep, I stand over him and shake myself, which wakes him up and makes him cross. Never mind, its time we were off anyway. I had awoken once during the night, when a strange man appeared in the doorway of the pillbox. Apparently we had his sleeping place for the night. I gave a quick bark and he soon hopped it to find somewhere else.

Heading now for Gt. Yarmouth George says we have now passed the most Eastern point of the British Isle, so it's now, onwards, North. We head for Hopton-on-Sea we see a golf course and a mass of holiday caravans, all lined up waiting for the summer tourists. After passing rows of fishermen, all under their umbrellas, we trudge on to Great Yarmouth. We cross Haven bridge when spot the Tan Lane Cafe and have a welcome cup of tea for George, with a big plate of egg and chips, and I had some dog food in a dish. We go to pay, and the cafe owner says "It's on the house" we both thank him very much, it has really set us up for the day, and then once more out into the rain and on with our walk.

George discovers a workman's hut, we decide not to break in. We find some scraggy grass for the tent site for the night, it will give us some protection anyway. George gives me the bone he was given earlier, and drinks his can of beer given by one of the fishermen. We are soon both fast asleep. Tomorrow we set off for Horsey, it will be day 49.

Awake at 6.30 the rain is pouring down. We have a quick breakfast and then pack up our gear. George says the tent is so heavy when it is wet, there is no way I can help him, except to stay close by his side and Wuff when spoken to. The sea is very rough and the big waves frighten me a little as they crash and race ashore, but George is with me and says everything is O.K. We move up to the sand dunes, a bit further away and continue to walk. We pass Horsey and eventually arrive at Palling. George and I meet some workmen sitting in their hut drinking tea, they tell us they are repairing the sea wall, needs it too, I thought. George gets a mug of tea, and me a scratch behind the ears and then we are off again. We are heading for Happisburg, we leave the coast and wander into the village. George posts his cards and gets a few provisions, which the man takes half price for and then we head for a little cafe. We both have a bite to eat and George gets his tea, and while we are chatting to the cafe owner and looking at the pouring rain, he suddenly says to George, that we are both welcome to stay the night. This is very kind and of course most happy to oblige as it is so wet outside.

George has a bath and sleeps in a double bed. I curl up on a nice thick rug, and we are soon oblivious to the weather outside.

Next day after a wonderful breakfast we are again on our way. The day is dull, but no rain yet, it can't be worse than yesterday, it was really the worst day since we had left home. And those waves they did frighten me, I kept a close eye on George, but I did prefer to walk a little further up from the bottom of the cliff where George was walking. We are going to try and reach Cromer to-day.

Mr and Mrs Eady who run the Seaview Cafe gave George £10 for the A.R.C. so we want to get to Cromer to get it into the post, and also to get to the Newspaper Office. The kindness of the Eady family was fantastic, and George had a wonderful breakfast, he hadn't stopped talking about it yet.

We head for the beach and turn left. All is well and we make good progress and seem to pass many miles. We arrive at Mundesley, so far so good. I remembered George reading about another man who passed this way only a few days ago, he had a dog too. Perhaps we are going to be pipped at the post, but we press on regardless. On passing Mundesley we note that the beach narrows, and the waves are a bit big again. However George ignores the footpath which leads up onto the cliffs and we continue on the beach, the miles pass and the wooden sea defences offer me a little comfort, until I note a landslide from the cliff blocking our way. George takes off his shoes and rolls up his trousers, picks me up because I was crying like a baby, and wades into the sea to round this mound of wet mud and earth. A wave hits us and we both tumble into the cold wet water. More and more landslips appear and I am really so scared, I know George is too. He clips me on the lead so as not to loose me, but the waves are huge and knock us over time and time again. George curses the waves, but they couldn't care less. We know what they can do to the remains of houses we have passed in the landslips,

so they certainly won't bother about us. George says
you won't have us yet and strikes out yet again around
another slide of mud. We see a beach again and stride
out for it when the waves have a last desperate bash,
knocking both George and I off our feet, we were out
of our depth and both have to swim for it. We
scrambled over a breakwater and sat on the sand
breathing deeply. We were so glad to be alive.
George said if we had drowned it would be rather sad
because no one would have bothered, and no one would
have known who we were.

We walk soaking wet along the beach when we meet a
young girl out with her dog, she says it is about a
mile to Cromer.

George and I head for the cliff path which is away
from the waves and much quieter. There I met a lady
who told George she was called Mrs Hines, she had
watched in dismay some of our antics in the sea and
said once we had reported to the Newspaper office to
come back to her house for a cup of tea.

We report to the newspaper office and arrange to come
back in the afternoon, and then we set off for Mrs
Hines house. George gets a nice meal and many cups of
tea, and I get a lovely meal too. Mrs Hines dries all
Georges things and she gives me a good rub with one of
her old towels. She is so pleased to do this she says
because she really thought we'd 'had it' and we were
sure to drown.

Much drier we set off for our appointment. The local
radio is not interested in our adventure, but the
local paper is, photo's are taken, and our story re-
counted and then we are off again northwards. I
collect a few more donations for the A.R.C. and then
we head for Sheringham, where we manage to find a Post
Office and get rid of the money. We find a shed to

sleep in and decide that we will take it easy tomorrow as well. It was quite a little escapade that we went through, and George and I still feel shaken.

We are now into the middle of April, the 20th to be exact and up to day 51. The sun is attempting to shine so George and I get up and set out for our days walk. We meet a nice chap out giving his dog a early morning walk, we talk about the possibility of the tide coming in or out and re-count our story of yesterday. We are invited back to his house for breakfast. Both he and his wife make us very welcome.

The sun still shines so we are off again, George is telling me about so many nice people in the world today, it makes us both feel so good that we are invited into peoples homes when they have never met us before.

We keep to the cliffs to-day, the going is slow because George will stop to talk to everyone we meet. We head towards Blakeney but take a small detour as advised by one of Georges new 'friends,' to avoid getting stuck on Blakeney Point. We pass a R.A.F. base and then head off across the fields to a path which runs past a bird sanctuary, we eventually arrived at the coast after George had done a spot of bird watching himself.

Wells, next the sea is our next point which according to the signpost is 8 miles from here. "We will look for a place to stay" says George," and we will have an early night" . Music to my ears, and I am eager to help him look. We see a bunker in a field, climb the gate, and shoo away some wild geese and settle in for the night. It's nice and dry, and we eat our supper listening to the rain and the wind. I kiss George Goodnight.

Last nights rain has stopped at last. It is however very cold and the wind is blowing, George wraps up well and grumbles about the wind. We cross the field towards the gate, avoiding the geese who don't seem in a good frame of mind, and reach the road. I see a huge worm trying to cross the road, I show George, who agrees the worm won't make it as the traffic is getting plentiful, so he gives him a quick lift on his boot and deposits him safely on the grass verge. The sun is shining this morning so perhaps we will make good headway, eventually arriving at Hunstanton, and George stops at a little grocers to stock up.

We are told by a man that we are now starting on 'The Wash' the wind still blows, I suppose you have to expect it on the East Coast. Heading for New Hunstanton we meet a lady who says she knows all about us, having read the papers and listened to the radio. She says George and I are a good team. George's head swells a bit more, and then another lady stops her car and comes over to talk to us. I still feel a bit tired, so I'm glad of a little sit down while George chats. We have a cup of tea, me drinking from the saucer in a local cafe, and George gets a bone for me. I will enjoy this for my supper.

We meet up with two men repairing the sea wall which we have just reached, they direct us to walk along the flood bank, which eventually will lead us to King's Lynn. We find a lady sitting in her garden and George asks if he could have a glass of water. She offers George tea, and he drinks a whole teapot full to himself. I get a pile of broken biscuits, she is ex-RAF so George is well away with his chatter, as of course he is ex-RAF himself.

After putting the world to rights we are once more on our way again,

We decide that it was time to look for a place to sleep. I see several rabbits, one would be nice for my supper. I nearly catch one, but he jumped down some sort of hole in the ground, I tried to follow, but I could only get my nose in, still never mind, there is always the bone.

George sees a barn that might be suitable for the night, so we have a quick gander, and decide it will be O.K. There is an owl in the corner who keeps hooting, but we manage to sleep through it, and awake fresh to a sunny morning.

Still continuing along our flood bank we eventually reach King's Lynn. We report to the Newspaper Office and then off again along the road to Boston. This road is very busy with lorries so George puts the lead on me, I hate it, but have no option. At least the road is pretty flat, but it is 31 miles to Boston.

George is eating sweets. I don't get one, although I ask now and again. Roadworks ahead, that means a long delay, George for certain will talk to the workmen and end up with a cup of tea sitting in their little hut. At least I get a rest and a biscuit out of the rain. After ages, we arrive at the Sutton Bridge and then through the village, before arriving at Long Sutton. We find a footpath taking us off the main road which pleases me, the lead is unclipped and another signpost says another 28 miles to go. When we get to within 17 miles George thinks we have both had enough for to-day, so we look for a resting place for tonight.

We see an old pub all boarded up, we nose around a bit and find an old outhouse which would suit us fine. I fall asleep right away, but George listens to his radio a bit while writing up his postcards.

I awoke at 2 am to the sound of heavy rain beating down outside. We are both lovely and warm, so I nod off again until 7 am.

Next morning we get going early. we are now, George says, in the County of Lincolnshire. Hoping to get beyond Boston to-day.

We pass several fields full of flowers, daffodils, tulips etc:- which George says makes our walk a bit brighter.

We meet some men who are a support group for a long distance walker who is raising funds for Stoke Manderville, we all have a good chat, and then I think to myself we could have a support team following us like that, but it was a bit late to think of that now, George passes his regards for the good effort that he had encountered and then we see a cafe not too far ahead. We can "hear the kettle boiling from here", George says. I cant think how, because my ears are better than his, and I don't hear anything. Still we plod on and he must have been right because we all have a good drink.

As we sit in the cafe the walker passes us, he looked in pain but didn't admit it. George and I caught him up and we all had a little chat. We wished each other well and then he hobbled off, going much faster than we were going, it looked to me like a walk of agony, again I was pleased I had four paws to lighten the load somewhat. We spot another barn not far away, it is full of farm machinery but George says we can still squeeze in. The forecast is for rain again to-night, and the forecast was right.

Day 55, nearly the end of April. I found a dead cat this morning and decided to have a go. It didn't taste too special, and George shouted at me when he found out what I was doing. I just thought it would save him getting breakfast for me, but I had some anyway. George says I will be sorry before the end of the day, and I was. But after being sick a couple of times I feel O.K. again now.

We head across the fens for Wainfleet, George finds a phone box so he puts a call through to Mum to say all is well. A sign for Skegness appears, it is about 5 miles away, so we plod on. On arrival at Skegness we find we can look across to Hunstanton from the sea front. We head for the newspaper office and a welcome cafe for George's cup of tea. A good natured lady gives me a bone, and George and she talk for about an hour before we decide to leave.

Skegness seems a very busy place. We'll have a quick look around, find somewhere to stay, and return to the little cafe again for our breakfast tomorrow morning.

CHAPTER 7,

Skegness to Hull.

After finding a shed where we settled in for the night, we are awoken by someone shouting "Is there anyone there" I growl in response. George shouts out and then this man goes and calls the police. A young copper, in a car, screeches to a halt and comes into the shed, he was a very sensible chap and took details of what we were doing and then pushed off. We dropped off to sleep again as no one had turned us out. Getting up at 7am we decided to head for the little cafe for our breakfast. Another nice juicy bone for me, and then after some minor shopping, and calling at the newspaper office, we turned our heads towards Sutton-on-Sea.

The rain soon made Skegness disappear from view as we walked the beach. The sea was quite rough and its continuous roar worried me a little, I kept well away from the edge. The sun at last comes out and soon we reach three men, repairing the sea wall, that seems to be all they do around here, it must be a full time job keeping the sea at bay. George chats for a while and gets directions of how to find Harry's mum, who lives around here somewhere, at Sutton-on-Sea. Entering the town we call in on a shop keeper who gives George final directions of how to reach High Gate Lane.

We find Harry's mum, followed by the much appreciated cups of tea and a good fry-up. I sleep after a drink of milk, George says its wonderful finding an oasis of civilization on our lonely walk. Harry's brother Stuart, comes in and we all sit around a nice warm fire discussing the details of the past few weeks.

Stuart and George take me and Candy, (his dog) for a little walk, I would rather have stayed home, but George insisted a little walk would do me good. We stay for the night.

Day 57 26th of April. The day is bright and after a good breakfast of porridge and scrambled eggs for George, and me a tin of Candy's meat, once more we set off. We say goodbye to Harry's mum and Stuart and thank them for their hospitality and cheer, and then George and I, feeling good, soon arrive at Mablethorpe. We call on a lady reporter who gives George Coffee and me water, and then calls up a photographer who takes our pictures, while she writes our story.

Time passes quickly and once more our noses have to turn North. Reaching the sea again we walk along on the sand dunes until we reach the main Grimsby road at Saltfleet, we walk along this for about a mile, when George meets a man who gives him directions along a track to the flood bank, we find the track and follow it. The R.A.F. own part of this area as an exercise area, we see a lot of aircraft, we arrive at Donna Noah nature reserve on our right, while on our left fields of young corn are in view. As we reach the sand dunes again the sun still shines, but the aircraft are still circling overhead, suddenly they start firing at targets on the beach. I've never been so frightened in my life, it was much worse that the waves rushing at us. I panicked and ran. I ran and I ran, until I couldn't breathe any more. In the distance I could hear George calling me, but I couldn't possibly return. I somehow didn't like the idea of being a moving target for them. I lay low. George tells me afterwards he couldn't have carried on without me, he was frantic with searching. All the interest for the walk had gone out of him, and he was in the process of returning home to Mum, but he couldn't leave me.

I heard later that he called into the local police house and told his story to the policeman's wife. After a couple of phone calls a Panda car came to pick him up and take him to the police station where he once more told his story about loosing me. The Panda car takes him around and they search the area, but no good. It is now dark and they had to give up for the day. A lady in her garden says she saw a dog answering my description heading for Louth. George sets off on foot to try and find me. It was dark so he looked for a place to stay, finding a barn he half slept and half dreamed, he told me afterwards that it was a very worrying time. He felt so lonely and although he loved me a lot, he realized that I meant all the world to him.

Next day at light he reported back as instructed to the Police. On the way George finds a phone box and calls Mum, she is as upset as he is and tells him to come home. However he must go on to find me, he will not leave the area until he knows what has happened.

He heads for Louth again and finds the Police Station there and reports his loss. Everyone is very kind and friendly and George sees a different side to the Police to what other people see. The police get in the local radio rep. and the local papers, as George is giving them all the details, the Chief Constable walks in and hears the story. "NOT ON MY PATCH you haven't" he says. He sends out a group of constables to search the area, muttering to himself, "no-one looses anything on my patch" he went into his office. Within about twenty minutes the news came through that I had been found in Louth. George was overjoyed and loved and kissed me, it was most embarrassing. Me, well as the darkness crept in I found a chicken coop.

I poked my nose in the door and found five or six hens sitting on their perch above me, they said I could come in if I was quiet, so I spent the night there, and that's where I was found by the lady who owned the hens the next morning.

I felt very ashamed at leaving George to his fate, but I really panicked, I hope he will forgive me.

The Policemen at the station made such a fuss of me. George said someone must be watching over the both of us, (other than the police). He really cared for me and thought he would never see me again. Cups of tea were given out at the police station, and someone was sent out to get a tin of dog food, which I gulped down in three big bites, well I was pretty hungry by then, having had no supper or breakfast.

The newsmen, the radio rep. the police all wave us goodbye and wish us well. Everybody has been wonderful. George says he knows what it is now to really worry when you care and love something you are responsible for. He gives me a quick pat and we decide we have had enough for to-day, we will look for somewhere to bed down and get over the trauma of the past twentyfour or more hours. We find a phone box and phone Mum to tell her I have been found, she is relieved, so alls well that ends well. We find a small forest and put up the tent. George seems as pleased as me that we are together again. We sleep in each others arms tonight. Tomorrow we set off for Grimsby, which George says is only four miles away.

Day 59. 28th of April. Both George and I slept for a full ten hours last night. We were so exhausted. Even the forest noises didn't wake me, although I sensed they were there. The forest is full of all sorts of bird life, the crows are nesting and making an awful screeching noise. The road nearby is now

'Picked up by the Police.'
Louth.

full of morning traffic, although two deers look on us
from a safe distance.

We set off for Grimsby at 8 am. having spent our first
night on Humberside. A man stops his van to say he
saw our picture in the local paper and wishes us well.
He gives me a dog chew, which I carry for some
distance before I eat it.

After George thanked him we continued on our way,
passing a few houses on the outskirts of Grimsby. It
was here that we met Mr Stuart Grant leaving home for
his work. It was he who came to George's help two
days ago when I got lost. He and his wife had read
the paper that morning, and they were so pleased I had
been found. Setting off again we avoid going through
Grimsby town and head off towards the Humber.
George's sixth sense leads him to a caravan selling
tea. We meet up with Don who is the owner, who makes
a big fuss of both of us. A really good chat by
George, food and cold drinks to take on our way and a
promise of a heatwave for next week.

I meet a customer at the caravan called Mr. West who
tells George to call on him when he reaches Hull. We
leave the caravan and continue North, I hear an
aircraft overhead and I cower in the grass. George
tells me it is O.K. it is a long way away, I still
feel very frightened about the noise. Perhaps one day
this fear will leave me but at the moment it is still
very near. A group of Industrial chimneys loom up on
the horizon, some with smoke coming from them. I have
never seen anything like this before and I look up
into George's face but he says it's "The industrial
North", whatever that means. Some of them have
visible flames coming out of them. I am not too sure
about all this and would rather go another way, but
George says its nothing to worry about. However I
still feel nervous.

We pass through Wooten village about 4 pm., and George says we will look for a place to stay the night. We see a barn, but it is in view of several houses so we decide to leave it and find somewhere else. The rain is falling hard as we head towards the Humber Bridge which is now in view, George says there is a cemetery close by and we will go to have a closer look.

We find a building with a door half open, it is a store of some kind so we decide this will do nicely. Personally I do not like these churchyard places, I always feel I have too much company at night.

I awake in the morning to find my head stuck inside of George's sleeping bag, The rain is pouring down but we have a quick breakfast, or at least I did. George said he had almost run out of food, I said he could share mine, but he gracefully declined. We will get more provisions in Hull, he told me.

The bridge is four miles away so through the rain we trudge, on arrival I was a little worried but decided the walk would not be too bad as we were a long way up from the water. It was a long walk but on reaching the other side, George spots an information van, he calls in and the lady explained to him where he was. On finding out what we were doing she makes George a cup of coffee and gave him a map of Hull and all the directions. I got a bit of chocolate, much to George's disgust. The local bobby called in as well, and he and George had a very enjoyable half hour chattering. We set out for the town centre and call at the local newspaper office. We do an interview and then cross the road to the local radio station.

The house we have been directed to was in a long road, and on ringing the bell of No. 58 find there is no-one at home. We, wait in the garage out of the rain, until the owners come home. Soon Dennis and Eileen

West arrive. They race around to feed their eight
cats, I don't think I'll bother to talk to them
myself, they might gang up on me. George stays the
evening watching the telly, but I have to stay in the
garage because of the cats. It's dry anyway. As
night approaches George comes out to get me and we go
to bed together, so all is normal.

Next morning we wait for all the cats to be fed and
out of the way before we come downstairs. Dennis
gives me a couple of addresses of friends of his at
Hedon and another at Witherwick who we can call on as
we pass by.

After a good breakfast we are on our way and say
Goodbye and many thanks for the hospitality we
received last night.

We cross the river and head for Hendon, George and I
meet a friendly milkman, they stop for a chat and
George gets a bottle of free milk which we share. It
was a bit of a job drinking out of the bottle so
George finds a small hole in the ground which he pads
out with mud, and I get a quick drink there before it
soaked into the ground. We arrive at Hedon and find
Dennis's friend, Mrs Pat Whitton waiting for us. Both
George and I get a good feed and then she gives George
food to take with him, we pop next door to meet the
neighbours, Mrs Aitken and her daughter Susan. Both
are nurses, another nice mug of tea and George and I
are off again northwards

CHAPTER 8.

Hull to St. Andrews.

George shouts to me to listen, he hears a cuckoo for the first time this year, its been the wettest April since records began his radio says, and I quite agree. It isn't raining at the moment but the mist is coming down, not very pleasant to walk in. It suddenly gets thicker and George clips my lead on, in fact we can hardly see our hands in front of us. We press on and look for a barn for the night, but find we have covered more miles than we thought and we are now entering Witherness. We find Mrs Longbothem's house, we meet her neighbour, a nice old chap who only has one leg. He makes such a fuss of me and I rather like him, we go into the house and sit in front of a nice coal fire while George watches T.V. Our friend next door is now at home, and invites us in but I'm fast asleep in front of the fire so I stay. George has a nice meal and cups of tea and a warm bed offered. He fetches me just before he goes upstairs, I am not bothered about supper to-night, I really am too tired.

Day 62. Its the first day of May, we get up at 6 am to listen to the rain on the window. George sorts through his kit for a lost tin opener. No breakfast for me I suppose. He thinks he left it behind in the cemetery, more likely the spirits took it, as I've said before, I'm not too happy about churchyards.

We have a good breakfast at 9 am. George borrowed an opener for my tin so I got breakfast as well. He says we will buy another to-day somewhere. We give our farewells and head for the coast again. We pass a Sunday Market and George buys a few sweets and a tin opener for me. The rain pours down and the wind blows in from the North sea. We were offered to stay a second night with Mrs L as the weather was so awful. We telephone back and we were told we would be very welcome, with this in mind we now head back to the warm fire and civilization for one more night.

We have a lazy next day and just go out for one little walk with Mrs L. and her dog Sheba, Sheba says I could live with her if I liked, but I thought I had better stay with George and thanked her for her offer.

The rain still comes, and the forecast says there is more on the way, we can stay tomorrow too if we wish, but we will decide this in the morning. Mum rings twice during the evening, once to give me an address in Scarborough, and later to correct an error she made in the address.

Day 63. The second of May. Not actually raining, but its looking like it any minute, however George says we really must start or we will get to like the softness of our existence at present. Before we go a local newspaper reporter calls with a photographer, so we tell our story once again. It's getting late so we stay for yet a third night in this wonderful house. Tomorrow we really must go whatever the weather. I have a lovely bath in a tub in the backyard, and George has a bath in the house, we all smell lovely and fresh. A friendly butcher gives Sheba and me a nice bone each and then I get some meat for tomorrow, what friendly people the Yorkshire people are. Everyone points to me as I walk along and chat with George, my back end is beginning to swagger a bit.

After another good night we get going again, to-day we are making for Hornsea, that is where, George says all the beautiful china is made. We are a bit behind with our schedule so we will not go to have a look. We reach Sand Le Mere, the aircraft are flying and I am a bit restless, we climb off the beach up the cliff to the top, when suddenly we hear shouts. Mrs L. has followed us by car to say the T.V. people are coming to do another story on us. We sit and wait and when they arrive we do our bit of acting again. After all I have had a bath this time, and you don't know what other dogs might be watching, I stretch my paw up over my face and push back my fur. I am ready. The camera team give George some money for the A.R.C. We shake hands and paws after a while, and with another cheerio to Mrs L. we set off again. The sea has really taken its toll of this coastline, with huge chunks of fields slipped down into the water, at one place the erosion has reached a farmyard, I wonder how long they have before it all disappears into the sea, it must be heartbreaking for the farmer and his family. We ease our way through a field of cows with only an electric fence to stop them falling over the edge. I keep well away from the fence and the cows.

The R.A.F. start to fly low and fire at targets at Cowden. George puts me on my lead but I am not happy at all, still we eventually pass by, we skirt the red flags flying and soon pass by Albrough. We climb down to the beach and after passing a group of soldiers out on manoeuvres we see eventually, Hornsea. It is early closing so not many people about. After a quick sip of tea in a beach cafe we head out of Hornsea towards Bridlington, George says we will hurry along as he sees that I am still scared of the aircraft. We climb back up on the cliff and find two bunkers in a field, they are both flooded, but in one there is just enough room to sleep on a dry patch at the back. We call it a day and close down about 7.30pm.

This morning it is raining, but George says we must get some food so we head for Saltburn, we stock up and ask directions to Redcar, we stop off at a little cafe, where the proprietors are Devonians. We

obviously stay longer than we should, and then George
and I are off again. George seems to feel a bit
homesick after our last stop, he says we must be mad
to do this walk, I've thought that for a long time,
but we have nearly as far to walk back as to go on
now, so we decide to persevere. We meet a man with a
funny looking dog, half a poodle and half an alsatian.
The dog is very friendly though, and he and I have
quite a chat until his owner nearly has a fit and
drags him off around a corner, we hear him screaming
at the top of his voice and throwing his arms around.
I thought,' Poor dog' I am glad that my master is more
or less normal, most of the time anyway.

We walk along the river Tee towards Middlesbrough, we
were supposed to meet a photographer along this route
from the press office, he must have fallen in the
water because we never saw him. Anyway we have to
hurry as George wants to be in Blythe by Thursday to
meet Martin. In the meantime we have found an old
shed to settle for the night. Next morning we get
going early, we have a long slog ahead on the busy A19
and see a sign for Sunderland, twenty miles or so.

Pausing at a tea caravan I am given a juicy beefburger
and George a plate of fish and chips, we do not have
to pay and with good wishes we plod on again. We have
a bit of rain and sleet and I feel very tired, George
says this is the second longest day we have walked.
Feels like it too. We attempt to walk through the
four miles of the Tyne tunnel. I am not particularly
fond of enclosed places, and to my delight George
discovers that pedestrians are not allowed. We are
directed to walk a little further on, through a
housing estate where we come to a second tunnel. A
man at the entrance puts George and I into a lift and
takes us down 85 ft. not a nice feeling at all.
Nearly as bad as the boat, we can then walk the four
miles, so we hurry through, we meet up with another

man at the other end who takes us back up to the
surface, where we head for Tynemouth. George says it
was in this area of South Shields that the lifeboat,
as we know it to-day, was first built. Also we're near
the area where our brave heroine, Grace Darling rowed
a boat, with her father (who was a lighthouse keeper)
on the Farne Islands, near Berwick, to rescue nine
seamen who were in danger of drowning.

This deed of gallantry was achieved through raging
seas and stormy skies, to rescue sailors from the
stricken ship 'Forfarshire.'

I thought of a little rowing boat in amongst those
giant waves and shuddered. This of course was in the
year 1838 and Grace was in her early twenties. How
brave she must have been. Perhaps the waves were not
as big then as they are now?.

She died at the very early age of 27 years.

George says that he is tired, I thoroughly agree
although I felt he was underestimating it a bit, we
look around for somewhere to rest tonight. There are
quite a few sheds with cattle in them, but one is used
just to stock the hay. We are in clover and do not
even attempt to eat any supper. Oh! I cant remember
feeling this tired before.

We both awoke at 7.30 the next day, our 72nd day, and
after breakfast we are on the road again.

We arrive on the seafront where I had a good run
around, its been a bit tedious being on the lead for
so long, but George said I must be patient, and this
is my reward.

George asked his way to Whitley Bay from a man out
walking, and he was told that this was Whitley Bay.

George is surprised, we meet up with the press people and then on our way again to Blythe.

George looks for a cup of tea, but no luck. I meet up with a dog called Bill, and have a bit of a play. Bill's owner, a very nice lady, invites George to her house for a cup of tea. After many cups of tea, and bowls of clean water for me we reluctantly say our goodbyes. After making enquiries George eventually finds Herringull Close in Blythe, I look up in the sky in case we get attacked by gulls, but all is clear. We find No. 24 to be greeted by Margaret's Mum, a wonderful tea and a hot bath. for George. When Martin comes home with Margaret, George and I and Martin head for a drink at the local pub. There was a drunken song in progress, so we all join in, even me, and then I had to lead both Martin and George home again, as I was not sure if they knew the way.

Next day we set off again along the sea front where we have some photographs taken. The sea is looking very black, most unusual I thought. It is quite rough and both George and I get wet when a large wave came over the sea front wall and drenched us. We pass a small church, right on the edge of the sea and then we have to cross a rough strip of very black land. This apparently, so George says, is an open coal mine. Its no wonder the sea is such a colour. We climb up over some coal mounds and then get back on to the coastal road at Lynemouth, arriving eventually at Creswell. After calling into the 'Plough' pub we find a place to settle for the night. I'm surprised that Martin has stayed with us, he was just going to walk a little way with us I thought, but he is still here at midnight. George and Martin erect their tents and I scramble in with George and we all chorus goodnight to each other.

Next morning after breakfast we make our way towards Amble, Martin has a pain in his knee, and after a few

more miles he is in agony. We stop at a little
village garage and ask to borrow the phone. George
phones Margaret to come and pick Martin up. She
arrives in the car, bringing a big thermos of coffee,
Martin is packed into the front seat and then we are
on our own again. We stop at Broomhill P.O. to get
some stamps to post George's cards. The Post Office
lady is not very polite and says dogs are not allowed
in her P.O. There is no notice outside, but all the
local people know. It takes all sorts to make a
world, George says, and he loves me anyway.

We find a barn to sleep in tonight and then off again
the next morning passing a huge rat who seems to have
spent the night with us and was now having his
breakfast of corn husks. I was not really bothered
about chasing him, I was still tired from yesterday.
We are twenty miles away from Berwick-upon-Tweed when
a little Poodle sidles up to me, stupid little
creature. She tries to have it off with me, but I am
not interested. She follows us for two miles, and
George does his best to get rid of her, but it was
only when we spotted an old hut on a railway siding,
that we both managed to escape. We had our dinner and
then watched some sheep in a field. One was wriggling
around on its back with all its legs waving about in
the air. George said it couldn't get up, I thought it
must be pretty old then, anyway George went into the
field and pulled and tugged the creature around until
it was able to get up. Our good deed done for the day
we packed our things and started to walk again.

We find a public call box, so George has a quick phone
call home to say all is well. The sun is shining for
once and we pass a sign which says nine miles to
Berwick. We post a card to Barry in Edinburgh to tell
him we are not far away, and then we look around for a
place to sleep.

Tomorrow we're on our way toward the border separating Scotland and England.

We have crossed the border into Scotland, we have now been walking 77 days. The sun is shining so George and I start singing "Oh, what a beautiful morning.' All the birds are disturbed and George says it is my voice, I have no tune, so we decide it would be best to stop. We see a phone box and ring Mum, to tell her we had crossed the border, she is still in bed but is pleased, and said Barry had rung, he had the card we sent and would expect us sometime. We head towards Eyemouth, not a lot of character here, George says, a lot of grey council houses, so we go on to Caldingham. I smell out a butcher's shop, I go in alone as George is some way behind, and queue up behind a lady. The butcher laughs when he sees George and me, and says he has been watching our progress on the Telly. He says I am well trained and as a treat I get the biggest bone I have ever seen, nearly too big to carry. Anyway George puts it in his rucksack for my supper.

He takes down our story as he says his son is a reporter, and then after a cup of tea we head for Dunbar.

Walking along five miles of very straight road we came across another man digging his garden, he had a dog called Shep, and I got on really well with him. He showed me all his secret places, and he said when I had finished this walk I could come back to him for a holiday. Meanwhile George had been invited in to the house and given more tea and a big fry-up of eggs and bacon. Mrs Turnbull packed George up a whole freshly made cake before we left. George and Mr Turnbull exchanged addresses, and we felt as if we were leaving long lost friends.

Much refreshed George and I set out to walk the rest of the long moorland road. We note it is thirty-seven miles to Edinburgh. We see a roofless house, George and I check it out and find that the old cupboard under the staircase which will just take the two of us, has a roof of sorts and is dry, so we both climb in and shut the door. I have a good long nibble of my very large bone, and then George puts it away for another day.

Next day it is raining as we head for Dunbar, we pass through and take the road to Whitchurch village, the way here is very pleasant with lots of forests on either side. The rain stops and a mist comes down, but not too bad. George and I stride out, this road is so pretty and part of it runs along the top of the cliffs by the sea, we pass a large castle which George says is Tantallon Castle and onto North Berwick. We pass through several villages and along a golf course road where we keep our eyes about us, just in case.

Just out of Aberlady we see a forest on our left. George finds a good place for the tent and we decide to call it a day. We both listen to the news on the little radio, and then close down for the night.

Next day, we set off on a wet road, although it has stopped raining for a while, which is good, George packs up his wet weather gear and I give myself a good shake. We look for a signpost to Dalkieth, and then as we pass a little garage we notice a tea machine where we can buy a cup, of course George cannot pass by so in we go. George also buys some more batteries for his radio, just in case, we then head for Mayfield, finding we are on the right estate we knock on the door to No. 48 and tell Barry we have arrived. George said it was good to see him again from his R.A.F. days, and after more tea and still more, they eventually paused to look at me. Well, I was bored silly, I was fast asleep on the rug. George and Barry went down the road for a pint, but I was quite happy to stay where I was.

George was up early this morning, and took a cup of tea into Barry to wake him, he said he had had too much frivolity last night, but after a quick look at his morning papers he took us both into Edinburgh for a guided tour. We call first at the Newspaper offices for the normal pictures and stories, and then a call to the local B.B.C. in Queens Street, then its off to see the Castle, all very impressive. We climb up the hill to' Arthurs seat' to look at the spectacular view over the city. The sun was shining and we really enjoyed sitting in the sun and resting at the top. A comfortable bed for the night and then we must once more get going. George and I take a slow stroll to the shops to stock up on provisions, and then its more goodbyes all round and we head off for Princes St. and the Forth bridge to continue our journey.

On arrival we walk across steadily, it is all very impressive and a really wonderful piece of engineering. I feel a little nervous, the water, however seems to be a long way down, but I am glad to reach the other side. We go down some steps and turn our noses towards Kirkcaldy and then Aberdour, we walk through the village and meet a friendly gentleman who invites George in for a cup of tea, which of course is not refused. The day George refuses a cup of tea, I know something is badly wrong.

That night. We find a barn in a little wood. There is plenty of hay inside, so we both have a good night and then wake up next morning to day number 84. Its lovely and sunny as we head towards Buckhaven. There are farms scattered on either side of this road and eventually we walk down the hill to St. Andrews.

CHAPTER 9

St. Andrews to Bonar Bridge

In front of us we see a nice sandy beach, George lets me have a bit of a run, I do enjoy rolling in the sand. The sun is shining and the newspaper office is pleased to see us. George meets up with Mike, a very pleasant reporter man. We both accompany him to the local pub, where George is treated to a pint, and I have a bowl of water. We enjoy a very nice meal on the house, and then after photographs, and George and Mike have exchanged addresses we carry on northwards. There seem to be a lot of aircraft about, but I've got more used to them now and stay by George's side.

George has acquired two ready-to-eat kippers for later, given to him by the radio lady, I'm not too sure whether I want to join him, they smell a bit to me. It's quite a way from his rucksack to my nose, but I stay close, and hope that supper will soon arrive and pass. Following directions, we eventually arrive at the Local Mental Hospital, and George says we must be lost. It's no good asking anyone around here for directions as they all seem to be barmy. Eventually we spot a sign for Abroath which says eighteen miles. We kip down in a forest for the night. When we awake we find posters nailed to all the trees, and they weren't there last night. The Scottish Nationalists must have been busy while we slept. George had his kippers for breakfast. I was pleased to see them go. The air is much fresher now.

We pass a butchers shop where George is able to get a bone for me, the lady in the shop tells us she has a brother living in Exeter, so with this information tucked under our belt we get a second bone for tomorrow, and George some brawn. We meet up with a

Salvation Army man, who invites us into the local hostel for a meal. In the hall a lot of people cheer us and make such a fuss of me. I get bits from all the tables, and I really feel very full. A good bowl of water finishes me off and I am soon asleep on the nearest rug. Jim McClusky goes to a lot of trouble to make us feel welcome, he takes a collection plate around for the A.R.C. and gives George a fabulous walking stick. He tells George he is being posted to Thurso by the Salvation Army, in the most northern part of Scotland, on the coast, so we hope to meet him again when we reach that far.

After fond farewells we set off once again, George has stopped at a sweet shop to buy a few sweets for himself, and a couple of cream ones which I like. He says he will not give me many as it will spoil my teeth. He doesn't say what it will do to his. Montrose is our next point to head for but at the moment it's pouring with rain, so George has had to stop to put on his wet weather gear. The first rain we have had since entering Scotland. A strong wind is blowing, which makes walking very difficult, George is glad of his walking stick.

We find an old deserted farmhouse with half a roof, although not ideal, George says it will have to do. I have my bone, and George his supper, and then we find a dry spot among some rubble to settle for the night. The next day the rain has stopped but the wind still blows, we have been walking for eighty-nine days now. George says we are a long way from home, I agree but what can I do about it. He has enough money sewn into his coat lining for our fare back to Devon, just in case. Mum put it there for an emergency, its nice to know anyway.

George soon perks up and I am sure he will soon find someone to talk to again, apart from me. A mouse shoots across the floor of the cottage, I glance at the creature but I am really too full to bother about it. Live and let live, I think to myself.

Arriving at Montrose, George finds a cafe for some tea. I find a fairy cake on the floor, so that soon goes, and then after buying some provisions and watching the wild ducks in Montrose basin we ask the way to John's Haven. On our way I spot a huge hare in a field, all my food has settled down and as I had room now for something else, I gave chase, but after seventy yards or so I gave it up as a bad job, I fell into a little stream and made myself all wet, but I do feel well after that scamper and soon rejoined George on the footpath again.

We have been directed to an old friend at a local school. This we find and there is also a dog called Susie who gets on well with me. Some of the girl dogs are quite stupid, but not Susie, she and I get on like a house on fire. George has a bath and a shave, and then after we meet the Headmaster, (a friend of Mark Stuarts), we all have a lovely meal and a warm bed for the night. I share a basket with Susie, she said it was big enough, but it was a bit of a squash.

Next morning we had breakfast with all the children in the school, and I got lots of tit-bits of course, apart from my proper breakfast. George was asked if he would talk to the children about our adventure. He did this with a lot of help from me, and then, as the Headmaster had taken such a fancy to George's walking stick, he gave it to him. All the pipe band turned out to give us a musical send off, so we left the little town in high spirits, with shouts and waves from the children, I would have preferred to just edge away quietly, without all that hoo-haa and screeching pipes, but George thoroughly enjoyed it. It is the last day of May to-day, so the weather should begin to

look up a bit, we press on towards Stonehaven. George
and I pass Dunnottar Castle, very impressive it looks
beside the sea and then down the hill overlooking
Stonehaven harbour. Passing through Stonehaven we
stop to watch a Tug-of-war on the seafront and then we
set off up another hill to Kings Gate, to see the
local T.V. people. The receptionist phones Ian Thorne
for George, a friend of Georges's from the R.A.F. He
comes to collect us and takes us back to his flat for
a bed and a meal. We meet the girl friend, and then I
curl up by the fire. Ian and George nip down to the
pub, and we are both persuaded to have a good rest and
stay for a second night. Wonderful, I didn't need
persuading at all. On the first day of June George
says we really must be off or we wont want to walk any
more, suits me, but he gets his gear on and after more
farewells its off towards Aberdeen. Christine, Ian's
girlfriend, and Ian wave us out of sight, after taking
us back to the picking up point.

We are entering our fourth month 'on the run' as it
were. It is June and the weather should be picking
up, but it still seems to prefer to rain. As we are
near to Aberdeen we spent last night with Gordon and
Catherine. She immediately told George to change into
Gordons spare things, and put all of his clothes into
the washing machine, and I mean ALL. I thank my lucky
stars for that, but before George has his bath, he is
told there is a big tin bath of hot water for me in
the yard. We all smell gorgeous after that, and we
spend a very comfortable evening before bed.

Next day we must be off So much for all the cleaning
up, it is still raining, but after more farewells,
packed lunches etc:- we are on our way.

We call at a local shop for supplies for me, and then
we follow a sign which says Peterhead, a car stops and
we are again offered a lift, but George explains we

have to walk. We pass several forests on the brow of a hill, we take note that Peterhead is another seventeen miles, so we quicken our step to try and put as many miles behind us as possible. The rain eases but the road is full of heavy lorries. We get honked at with hand waves, and I howl in reply. I don't much like this honking business. A very nice broad Scotsman stops his car and gives George a can of Ale. I hope he doesn't drink too much of it while he is walking, or goodness knows where we shall end up, I can't really put the tent up myself to cover him, but if I have to I will have a good 'go.'

We pass a whole heard of highland cattle, very impressive, George says. I am not so sure, to me they look as if they are Canadian Bison that have got loose. I really don't like the look of them, they have their heads right down and great big horns. I change sides with George and stay on the safety side. I walk quicker and quicker to put space between us.

We find a large shed, which seems at one time to have held about three or four houses. We have a roof over our head, we are about one mile from Peterhead. We eat and I get one of my juicy bones that George got for me in Aberdeen and then its a good nights sleep for two very tired creatures.....

We head this morning for Fraserburg, we pass St. Fergus and its huge Gas terminal and we stop for a chat to another Scotsman who directs us to a lovely clear stream, where George is able to fill his water bottle, and I get a lovely long cool drink. We stop at a local Post Office for George to post his cards, we buy some milk and a few sweets, we get all this for free as the people at the post-office refuse to charge us, very nice of them. I am taken to meet Georgie in the back, but we don't have a lot in common, so I return to George's side.

We meet a representative of the press who gives George a flask and a glass. However George finds that this is too much to carry, so reluctantly he gives it to the Postmaster, who then gives George some money for the A.R.C. I suppose that is one way of doing it. After a cup of tea for George, we are on our way again. I would not be surprised if I woke up one morning and found that George had turned into a teapot. In the meantime we trudge onwards when a little car stops by our side and a voice says the magic words to George. "I am called Jim, would you like to come to my house for a cup of tea? I will bring you back to this spot again to continue your journey afterwards."

We scramble into his car and after being made welcome by his wife, several cups later and with a haversack full of home-made goodies, we are returned to our original spot to carry on once again. I have had a nice snooze, and George has a full tank.

After a night in yet another barn we awake to a sunny sky. We are going to try and reach Cullen to-day. The road is very quiet this morning, I chase something moving in the grass, something Scottish, no doubt, they look, whatever it is, like some foreign animal to me. Suddenly a large head appears on the end of a great long neck. I squeal with fright and run back to George who says it is only a grass snake. All I can say is they are a lot bigger than the ones I have seen in England. He had red eyes too. Although George says I am imagining things.

The countryside is beautiful here, with forests and lovely green fields. It is Sunday when we arrive at Portsay. We met a nice lady on her way to church, she shows us a short cut through a park, she says she would have invited us back for a cup of tea if she'd had time. We thank her nicely, as George says, we

were at least pleased that we had been offered one,
although we didn't get it. We phone Mum at a call
box and we both have a good chat until George tells me
to shut up. After George has had an ice cream, which
I only got as a bit on the end of his finger, a good
sit down in the lovely sunshine we are off again
towards Portknockie.

We walk along by the harbour, which is quite pleasant,
and then up the hill to Portknockie. There is hardly
anyone about. The houses are small but well-built,
through the village and on towards Findochty. We stop
and chat to a lady sitting outside of her house in the
sunshine, I lay full length in the long grass and hope
the talking will go on for quite a long while yet, but
no. I do get a drink, and George gets a re-fill of
his water flask and then with a whistle he calls me
and we make our way down the hill to Buckie. This is
a seemingly endless town, and George and I seem to
take forever plodding through it, we eventually see
the sea and an old house in ruins. On investigation
we think it will do for the night. I stay outside in
the warm sunshine until George calls me in for supper.

After our morning duties we set off from our house at
Spey Bay towards Losiemouth. I don't feel so well to-
day and left half of my breakfast. George looks at me
worried but after I have been sick, (probably the newt
I ate from the last pond) I am O.K. again. We are up
to day 98 and the sun is still shining, for a change.
It looks like another warm day. We stop for some
water at a pub. The lady wasn't sure she would let
George have any, and then decided that he should pay
for it. However after a lot more talking, George got
it for free, and I even had a bowl of water. free.

We take the main road heading for Inverness. It is
quite pleasant with lovely countryside all around,
including Speymouth forest.

We get a few provisions as we pass through a little village. We chat to two workmen as we pass who are having their lunch, George gets a cup of coffee offered to him, and I get a bit of the sandwich, I could have done with all of it, but George told me not to be so greedy. We eventually arrive a bit in-land at Elgin. We find the newspaper office, where George does an interview with a reporter. George and I pass a fish and chippy. I said Pass, but we couldn't resist the smell. We go in and have fish and chips twice, a cup of tea, a bowl of water. After that we are fit again to find the road back to the coast at Lossiemouth. On the road to Burghead we pass a lovely forest, so many trees for a three-legged run-about. George says it is a lovely day and the weather for tomorrow is supposed to be good, so we will sleep tonight in the open air. I chase off a couple of deers who came to investigate us, and the little stream beside us lulls us into a gentle sleep as it chatters over the stones.

CHAPTER 10

Bonar Bridge. to Wick

It is the eighth of June, and we have been walking for one hundred days. It seems years since we left home in Devon. I can hardly remember my nice basket with a cushion in it. I do hope no-one else has taken it. However the sun is shining, and we are enjoying our walk, more or less. George has a cold, I hope he doesn't give it to me. We put our noses to the ground and head off for Nairn, we've travelled about seven miles, when George stops at a friendly looking house for a water re-fill. Of course he gets tea as well, and also a bath. He says it was fantastic, after more tea and biscuits we say our farewells, and especially to Clowey (a very friendly dog who I liked) and covered the three miles into Nairn.

George asks a Lollipop man the way to the newspaper office, and after buying a pot of jam at a little shop, we report in and stories are recorded and pictures taken we head off for Fort George. George sees a lovely forest which would do us for the night, but he says it is too early yet to think about sleep so we go on. Further on a small group of trees look inviting, so we stop. The forecast for to-morrow gives rain so George says we will erect the tent. I suddenly spot a large labrador type dog and I growl a warning. However Gemma is quite friendly, so while George and the lady owner have a long chat, Gemma and I have a run-about. By this time Mary, Gemma's owner was getting on famously with George, and when I saw him packing up the tent, I knew we had made it for another night. Mary had invited us both back to her lovely old farmhouse for the night. George is getting a real expert in his powers of persuasion, I am very pleased to say.

We meet George, Mary's husband, (I thought we would get a bit confused there with two Georges) but Mary seemed to be able to sort things out. George has three cups of tea and then two pints of George's home brew, I thought Oh, golly, I am going to get sung to to-night as well, but I needn't have worried, after a wonderful bath, George was soon fast asleep in bed, while I had a nice blanket on the floor. George really appreciates a good bed, he says it is one of the things he will never take for granted anymore. After a jolly good Scottish breakfast, George and I can hardly walk, we say Goodbye to George and Mary, and I have a quick kiss with Gemma. I did tell her if I was ever this way again, I would call and see her. We then turn our noses towards Inverness.

We do the newspaper bit on our arrival, stories and photos, it gets a bit boring at times, but George says we must do it. This photograph session seems particularly long, and I have an attack of diarrhoea, which George says was the dead rabbit I couldn't pass on the way to Inverness. Anyway all in all everything gets done and we start off again. We soon cross over a bridge to the Black Isle, and George stops for a cup of tea at a roadside van. We head on around the Black Isle, it is beautiful country here, with plenty of trees for me to play among. We stop at a village Post Office for George to phone home, and get some cards and stamps. The Postmistress makes a fuss of me, and has a long chat with George, we then head out of this nice quiet village and find a shed nearby that will do nicely for the night. We feed, lay out the sleeping bag and we are soon asleep.

Next morning we follow the coast road which runs beside the Moray Firth, the water looks pleasant, however we make steady progress and soon arrive at Cromarty after passing through woodlands of bluebells and wild flowers. All very pretty. George sits on a grassy bank for a while, and I'm glad of a little rest too. We must press on George says and stop admiring the scenery, it's a long way up and down these inlets. We could take a ferry across now and again, but George says this would be cheating. We stop at a house for a re-fill of our waterbottle, and after unpteen cups of tea from a lady who turns out to be a health visitor, and the story of our adventure so far, we once again set out, with good wishes ringing in our ears. I do hope the Scots people will not think too badly about George and his eagerness for cups of tea, but he says they are so welcome, he didn't know how much he missed them until he started this venture.

We are at the moment on the banks of the Cromarty Firth, the water is calm, and George and I walk a mile or two looking for a shelter for the night. The rain comes and I skirt very warily around a group of highland cattle. They have long hair, and longer horns, and I am sure their eyes are red. I don't much like the look of them and think they would be safer behind bars. I creep past them with my head low, perhaps they wont see me. George spots a small beach with one lone beach hut. We make our way towards it, and find the door is open with no-one about. It is empty so we both climb in out of the rain, there are a few holes in the roof, so George finds a couple of old plastic bags in the hedge and does a quick roof repair job to stop the rain coming in, and soon we are comfortably in the land of nod.

Next morning I awake to find George washing his socks in the Cromarty, and soaking his feet. He says they feel good now. I have a quick paddle, then it's breakfast and pack up our gear. We pass by Balblair and head towards Dingwall. We hit the A.9. and there is quite a bit of traffic which I don't like, George clips the lead on to me again, and we edge our way

along this very busy road. As the traffic eases we
make our way to Evanton, George unclips me and for no
apparent reason I chase across the road. A car hits
me and I fly through the air and tumble head over
heels into the long grass. I can hear George calling
me but I was so frightened I start heading off the way
we have come. I do not stop until I am back at the
Brigehead and heading back to Dingwall.

George is frantic and two Germans in their car stop to
help him. They don't understand him, but they already
have a hitch-hiker, Andrew, on board who interprets..
They take George to the Police station and Andrew
offers to help him look, after giving all the
descriptions. However a very nice chap called Bernard
has found me having seen some of what had happened and
arrives at the local station with a very shamed-faced
ME in tow, and says "Is this your dog"? to George.
George and I are so pleased to meet up again. I said
how sorry I was, and George and Andrew said they fully
understood. We all had a cup of tea to celebrate.

Bernard runs a christian home for children, and they
were on their way to a Victorian fete at a local
village. Andrew and George and I climb aboard
Bernards bus and meet some of the children who make a
fuss of me. I have one or two bad bruises on my side,
but on the whole I was very lucky. We have a
wonderful time at the fete, everyone was dressed in
Victorian gear except for George and Andrew. I of
course was O.K. dogs looked the same in Victorian
times as they do in the modern world. Andrew and
George and I are invited to spend the night at the
children's home, so amongst all the excited children
we have a safe haven for to-night. We all get a nice
welcome, have tea at long tables with the kids, I
found sitting underneath the table is very rewarding,
and then we three go for a little walk around the
village.

Next day is Sunday and George says he fancies going to Church with the kids, Andrew seems a very easy going chap and says he'll join George on the walk for a few days. I'm still a bit sore and scared, but I think George will really enjoy Andrew's presence, especially as he now has someone, other than me, to talk to.

The three of us are invited to stay at the childrens home for yet another night. So with good food inside us and well rested we start off again on our way to Invergordon. George meets up with an old friend, Bob Adams and his family, before we left the area. With Andrew accompanying us the miles seemed to go by quickly. We soon reach Invergordon where we get a few provisions and a bone for me. We are heading for Bob's house (another Bob) at Barbaraville. A very good friend of George's. We all arrive eventually and are offered to stay for a whole week. George says it is a bit long to encroach on Bob, his wife and baby Paul, and he will have to think about it. I am all for it, it sounds a wonderful idea to me. George phones Mum from the house and she sends her love to me and hopes my bruises will soon get better. We all have a good feed, and then George and Andrew get their sleeping bags out and kip down on the sitting-room floor.

The rain lashes outside, and I for one, am pleased we have a roof over our heads. The next day, George says he would like the local doggy doctor have a look at me, just to make sure all was well. Bob takes us in his car. Mr McIntyne is very good, he gives me a thorough examination and doesn't charge George a penny. George phones the local radio station and does an interview over the phone from the surgery. Andrew gets some provisions and then we drive home to Bob's house. After chopping some logs for Bob, and many more cups of tea, we again find the night has arrived. We decide that we really must get going again in the morning or we would get too soft.

The sun shines the next day so we say our fond
farewells and all three of us set out again. At the
end of the lane George turns and waves to Mary, and
then we reach the A.9. once more to head northwards.
We stop at a little shop for provisions. The lady
serving seemed nervous of George and Andrew, I can't
think why, they had a shave and a bath yesterday.
However we are on our way again to Bonar Bridge and
eventually Dornach. The countryside is really
beautiful, I wish we could only stay longer to enjoy
it. We pass a bus shelter and have a little sit-down.
Andrew phones his home in Glasgow, and George phones
Mum. All is well so we decide to find a sleeping
place for the night. We find an old church but it is
all locked up, we then see a shed, which by the smell
is usually occupied by a flock of sheep. Andrew
turned his nose up, but George would have stayed, but
then almost at Bonar Bridge George spots an old
bunker. George and I check it out. It's large and
dry, so in we all go. After a quick supper we are all
soon fast asleep.

George awoke at seven, but lay in his sleeping bag
until 9 am. I think both he and Andrew are worn out
with all this entertaining. Anyway eventually we all
get on the road again. Bonar Bridge is only about a
quarter of a mile away, but you can hear the traffic
from here. I did suggest to George we could swim the
river, but George clips on my lead and he and Andrew
set off with me between them. We soon pass over the
bridge and walk down the road around Donoch Firth.
The scenery again is wonderful, gorse bushes with
yellow flowers blending in with the forest greenery.
I did have a sniff at one of the flowers, but I
wouldn't advise it to anyone else, I got quite a nasty
prick on my nose, and George just laughed. George
says the hills he passes seem like mountains. Too
many soft beds for him lately. Andrew says they are
hills however, as they are under 3000 feet.

We stop at a little village shop at Spinningdale.
George asks for a re-fill of his water bottle, but the
man behind the counter refuses, and says he hasn't got
any. George asks him what he drinks and he says milk
or squash. We both wonder what he washes in, if he
does. George is very annoyed and although we are low
on provisions, refuses to buy anything in his shop.
Its not a bit like the Scots people we have
previously encountered. We call at a house just
across the road, Mrs Fraser, the owner is
exceptionally nice, and gives George all the water he
needs and apologizes for the strange 'goings on' at
the shop.

Andrew and George go on up the hill, and resolve to
stock up in the next village. Andrew points out two
buzzards circling overhead. I keep my head low.
Eventually we arrive at Dornoch, stock up and then
look for a place to spend the night. Andrew and
George eventually spot an old castle. We climb up
through the stinging nettles to investigate further,
and find what might do for a comfortable night.
Andrew gets a small fire going to cook himself some
food. It keeps the flies away, and I am pleased to
see also a mass exit of spiders. After this we all
settle down to sleep.

Next day, day 110, we set off again down through the
nettles and along the coast road until it joins the A
9 once again. It is reasonably quiet to-day. the sun
is warm and the countryside looks good. We skirt
around Loch Fleet and head on towards Golspie. This
town is quiet and quite pleasant. We stop for
provisions and a bite to eat and then head for Brora.
We pass fields of young lambs all playing in the
sunshine. We pass a huge monument of the Duke of
Sutherland, all very impressive. A young rabbit hops
out and crosses the road in front of us and I give
chase. George yells, I have to cut short my gallop

and retreat to the correct side of the road, then just ahead of us we see Dunrobin Castle, we pass by and then at the next village we all stop at the Fountain Cafe for a pot of tea. The people who run it are very nice, and offer us the shed at the back for the night. We are all pleased. After tea we wander down to the beach. George and I go for a paddle, while Andrew cleans up an old bottle he has just found. We chat with an local who tells us we have not got so far to go before we can call on Mr & Mrs Jenkins. The founders of the A.R.C. who only live about eight miles away at West Clyne.

We return to our shed, Andrew has bought a fish supper for himself, George is not that hungry but I have a big bone to myself. We all bed down at 8 pm.

We awake next morning to a crow making an awful din in the tree above our shed. We breakfast in the cafe, say our goodbyes to the owners and head for West Clyne. We follow a little grassy track and I give chase to a stray sheep and am severely reprimanded by George. That is one bad habit I must not start George says. Eventually we pass through an iron gate into the garden of Garty Lodge.

The house is really magnificent and we spot Mrs Jenkins sitting, enjoying the sunshine, while Mr Jenkins mows the lawn. They both look splendid people who make the three of us very welcome indeed. We all have a good chat, they told George they had almost given him up for lost, but I thought to myself here we are turning up like a bad penny. We all have a very nice Lunch, followed by oodles of hot tea. Mr Jenkins then takes lots of photos of us. George and Andrew are then offered home-made wine, followed by sitting around a lovely log fire. Supper and then bed for the night. Next morning its hot baths and breakfast.

Andrew says cheerio to-day and heads back to the main road to try and cadge a lift back to Glasgow. That means George and I are on our own again. I do miss Andrew, and I am sure George does too. Mr Jenkins has spotted a swarm of bees down on his vegetable patch. He is going to try and catch them. George offers his help, but I am too wise and sit with my nose between my paws just watching. I think about Andrew, he has a 250 mile journey to go to get to Glasgow. I wonder how many miles it is to Devon.? I am staying one more night with George at West Clyne, we can then meet the local press with an update of our story. George does the necessary interview and photos are taken and then its supper and bed.

Next morning there is quite a heavy mist over the sea, but we head downstairs for a massive breakfast, which George rounds off with five cups of tea, and then once more we are on the road heading for Helmsdale. Neither George nor I were very keen to move on as we both enjoyed the kindness and hospitality of Garty Lodge and the people who live there. The two dogs and the cat walked part of the way with us, and then headed back to their home, knowing full well where their comforts lay. I have a new bell attached to my collar, a present from Garty Lodge, so that George will know where I am.

We reach Helmsdale about noon and cross the new road bridge into the village. We get provisions and then head out and up to a new forest of Fir trees, young enough to still look beautiful. We then pass large patches of moorland as we head north, and great clumps of heather, and then we drop suddenly into Berriedale village. As we climb the hill the other side, George and I note the many crofters cottages along the way. We stop to chat to some crofters who are in the middle of sheep shearing. George gets a can of beer. Further on we meet three children, David, Catherine and Lorna and their mother. They have heard our broadcast on the radio, and invite us in for a cup of tea. On then to find our sleeping place for the night. Further up the road, George and I find an old shed with a roof on, unlike many of the other buildings we have passed along this road. Bails of hay are stacked at one side, but George says it will make a good sleeping place.

We sit outside for a while as we are near to some croft cottages. The owners see us and come over and give their permission to stay in the barn for the night. We are invited to share their supper before turning in, and then we are invited to stay the night in their croft on the sittingroom floor. It really was nice of them. After a very lazy evening, we have a wonderful nights sleep.

Next morning we say good-bye to Mr & Mrs Gunn, Adam and Eve to their friends, and following Adam's directions we head out for Dunbeath. We walk by mature forests with carpets of ferns and bluebells. George stops at a village Post Office for his supply of cards and stamps, and then its off down the hill, past the school where I meet some of the children. The sun has come out and the mist has lifted, promises to be a nice day.

We are told by a lady that it is only about fourteen miles to Wick. We have made good progress to-day. A little breeze has started up which eventually gets quite cold, almost galeforce, so we decide we have had a good innings and we will look for a place for the night. In the meantime George is offered yet another cup of tea from a lady Crofter, which he can't resist. He says the Crofters seem such a contented lot of people, and all of them look healthy. Now a large black cloud shows up on the horizon. We hurriedly look for our shelter for the night before the rain starts. We spot a derelict Crofters hut. It has a complete roof of heather stalks, covered by wire netting. George says this will be fine for us. I chase off several rabbits who all make it to their respective holes. I try to dig one out until George yells at me. Live and let live, he says. We have our supper, and while George listens to his little radio, I sprawl out on the floor and soon go fast asleep.

The rain was lashing all night, George said, but we were nice and dry. It has stopped now and we pack up our sleeping things and make ready for off. We are six miles from Wick, we stop for a quick chat with a donkey who has his head poked through a fence looking at us. I wasn't too sure to begin with, but it didn't have any horns sticking out so I passed the time of day with him. The land is very flat here, which makes for easier walking George says.

We pass through Thrumster and its many cottages, and eventually arrive on the outskirts of Wick. We report to the newspaper offices and then George asks directions to meet old friends of his by the name of Mr & Mrs McDowall. We find the right house and George rings the bell. Mr. McDowell answers in his pyjamas. George has got him out of bed as he had just come off his night shift. George gets several cups of tea waiting for Mrs McDowall to come home from shopping. Meanwhile George and Mr. M. have put all the world to rights and he has gone back to bed. George reads six letters which have arrived at the house and are waiting for him, then he has a hot bath and a shave and is decent once more. We are invited to stay the night and then we will tackle the final miles to John o' Groats in the morning.

CHAPTER 11.

Wick to Cape Wrath

Awakened by Mr. McDowell at 8am with a cup of tea for George. George is not used to this and I hope he will not get too soft. A lovely hot breakfast for both George and I and then after watching the boats in the harbour we are once more off.

Eventually George and I arrive at: JOHN O' GROATS.

The east coast is completed, George wonders what the rest of the country has in store for us. I wonder how many miles we have covered, it must be about 3,000 and it has taken us 116 days. We are not, George says quite halfway round yet.

George stops for some cash from a local Post Office, he tells the lady what we are doing and she says, "Yes, we get all the barmy ones up here." George laughs, but I wasn't too sure what she meant. A lady in her car passes and stops. "I have a tea Caravan about half a mile up the road", she said, "there is a free one waiting for you." I have never known George move so fast, and I go at a gentle trot beside him.

Passing the half mile in record time we spot a van which says 'Eat well with Rhona', and by golly, did we. A young cyclist called Duncan drops by, and George and he have a long chat. He is heading for the Youth Hostel, while George says we will spend the night in the barn, just a bit up the road.

Next morning we are awakened by Duncan, calling. The Youth Hostel warden wants to meet you and Jack. I told him all about meeting you and as we are all Ex-RAF we could spend the day chatting. So off we go.

Not only is he Ex-RAF, but apparently, Neil (The warden), Duncan and George were all at the same base for their square bashing at Swinderley, and the same Sgt. was in charge of them all. Needless to say with all that talking, we all had a fine meal, and George had a bed for the night, as it was far too late to get going again.

Next day Duncan told George that if he liked he would walk with him as far as Cape Wrath. Wonderful news for George, he would now have someone to answer him as well as talk to. We all set off about 9.30 a.m. and walk down to the main road again. We pass through East Mey and along the coastal road with the Atlantic Ocean on our right.

We walk around Dunnet Head towards Thurso. We hope to call on Lt. Jim McLusky, but unfortunately he is not in, (he was the Salvation Army Officer, George tells Duncan, that we met a long time ago). We wait around for quite a long time and then we put a note through his door to say we had called and continued on our way to look for our sleeping place for the night.

We find a barn and Duncan makes a big can of coffee. George really appreciates this as he hasn't had coffee for a long time. They chatter a lot but I manage to get to sleep, when suddenly I wake up with a growl. There is a large rat by Duncan's head, he wakes suddenly and pulls his bag nearer to George. A second very large rat appears, I don't much fancy chasing them myself, they look too vicious. George pulls one of the hay bales over a big hole when he had managed to chase them down, he calls me a coward, and we all drift off to sleep again.

We decide to make an early start, especially as the sun is shining, so once more we head off along the road to Strathy Point.

We pass by the Nuclear Power Station at Dounreay. I hurried past you never know when these things are going to blow up, then we head down the hill towards Reay. A lone cyclist pulls in to have a chat with us. He introduces himself as David Leighton, the second man to have walked the coast of Britain. He is equally pleased to see me, and says I will be the first dog to have ever done it (if I do), and my name will go into the Guiness Book of Records. I ruffle out my collar fur, and mumble,' Who says I can't?' We all sit down for a long chat, and Duncan makes us all some coffee.

I gingerly walk over a cattle grid as we head out onto the moorlands once again. I took it carefully as I know they can hurt your toes if you don't watch out. We have got a re-fill for our water bottle at last, so George says we will look around for a place to stop and have one of Duncans nice cups of coffee. We find an old empty house, and George checks around the back. There is an outhouse big enough for all of us. We pack everything in, in is like a party with all the chatter. Duncan gets his fire going in the old fireplace, boils the water and makes the whole place nice and warm and smokey. We all close down, utterly worn out with talking at 10 pm. I wuff wuff to them all but they are all fast asleep, too tired to answer.

A strong wind blows all night, but we all get up about 8.30 am. We head towards Strathy, the first of the five villages we hope to pass through to-day. We cross more moorland and note that the hills are getting higher. We progress westward along a narrow one track road. A cyclist stops by and says he has seen pictures of George and I in his newspaper this morning. He tells me that he has a dog called Bess, similar to me. We all look at the large breakers rolling in off the Atlantic. It is a most impressive, wild place with hardly anyone else to enjoy it but us.

Long stretches of golden sands, tufts of greenery here and there, and sea, waves as big as a double decker bus. I am happy to stay on the road and just watch them from there.

We approach Bettyhill village where we meet a lady out with her collie dogs, driving sheep. George notes the complete control she has over her dogs and says to me to take note, and watch. She chats to me while her two dogs sit obediently nearby. We get supplies at the next village, and George sees a sign for Tongue. We progress slowly, having said goodbye to David, Duncan and George seem very tired so decide to have an early night. Coming to a spot of moorland, they both erect their tents for the night. Duncan brews up, then we all turn in at 8pm. We awake at 3 am to the sound of heavy rain on our tent flap, another wet day for tomorrow I suppose.

We get up at 8.45, and we are happy to note that the rain is now just a misty drizzle. We pack all our gear, and we are off towards Tongue at 10.30am. George says he notes that our starter time is getting later every day, I did say to him he shouldn't do so much talking at night, it keeps me awake, leave alone him and Duncan. Its all Duncan's fault, he has this little stove, and any excuse is good enough for him and George to have a little rest with a CUP OF TEA. Men, they should be content like me with a drink from a stream. We pass through spectacular scenery with hills of mountainous size to George and Duncan. It certainly is pretty here, with no-one to spoil it and leave their litter. We pass through the small village of Coldbackie and then on to Tongue.

We do note the Kyle of Tongue away on our right. That is our next point of arrival, but in the meantime George and Duncan have got the little stove out again and they are making coffee.

George looks at his map and says there are only two villages between Tongue and Durness, a distance of thirty miles, we cross the water and get going on the Kyle of Tongue. The drizzle has now turned to heavy rain and both George and Duncan are soaking wet. Not only the rain but the wind gets up to gale force and every step we take forward the wind knocks us two back. After a few miles the wind and rain get even stronger and it is a job to keep walking. The men are both miserable, me included, this is no life for a dog, leave alone man. Duncan is now very fed up, and I think at one stage I could see him heading back to Tongue. However George spots a small building over the next hill, he urges Duncan to keep going, but he slows right down. It's getting very cold and he has almost had it. George climbs over a wire fence and investigates and then comes back for Duncan. He is almost at a standstill, George and I get him inside and then George goes back for his bike. Duncan goes immediately to bed to get warm. George feeds me and then gets out the little stove to make hot coffee for him and Duncan. I flake out on the floor, George has dried me with an old towel, he says he must get into his sleeping bag as well as he feels so cold. The wind roars outside, but we are all O.K. for the night.

After a restless night we all get up at 9.30a.m. We walk beside Loch Hope and Duncan feels a little better, the wind is still strong but the rain has stopped. I chase a few stray sheep, but George is not happy about this, but I have mastered how to get across the cattle grids we come to, so that solves the problem of having to be carried. At the far end of Loch Eriboll we start up the opposite side. We stop to fill the water bottle from a fast flowing stream. The road is much flatter this side, and makes for easier walking, we arrive in the far flung village of Laid. We spot an empty house, it is only just 3.15 pm. but George thinks Duncan has had enough, and a good rest for everyone is badly needed. We settle in with constant streams of hot coffee. George tells Duncan how much he and I will miss him when he goes when we do eventually reach Cape Wrath, but he says it is his stove and hot drinks that George will miss, and we heartily agree that he is right. Three people on bikes try the door of the cottage, I see them all off, obviously they are looking for a sleeping place too. After a few more hot drinks, George and Duncan kip down at 9.30pm. I wake up George at 7.15 am by putting my cold nose into his sleeping bag. Duncan is already up. We have breakfast and drinks and leave the cottage about 9 am.

We head towards Durness, the road is easy going and we make good progress. I chase a rabbit, but he got away as usual. Durness is a long village, we manage to stock up on provisions again and ask for information about the ferry to the Cape of Wrath. We decide to try and catch the 1 o'clock ferry so hurry the last one and a half miles, but when we arrive at 1.10 there is no-one in sight. George and I sit by the ferry post while Duncan ferrets around. Soon a red-faced ferryman appears from the local pub, shunts us all into his little boat and starts the mile long trip across the Kyle of Durness. The boat lurches from side to side as the ferryman tries to steer a straight line. I lay between Georges feet motionless, I feel sick, I do not like these boats. George and Duncan get a quick drink of Oxo on the way across by the ferryman, George says it was very welcome.

On arrival at the other side, Duncan, George and I start a long trek up a steep hill into what seems a wilderness of bleak desolation. All is quiet everywhere, with just a scatter of munching sheep, there are no other signs of life as we walk along this grassy track.

The mist turns to rain as we pass an old empty croft. We try the door, it is unlocked so we go in and make ourselves comfortable for the night. The place seems to be like a rescue H.Q. with kitchen, bunk beds and running water. We are surprised at our find and our good fortune, we needed to be rescued at this precise moment. Food is prepared in a civilized manner, Duncan lights a fire, we find a tin of soup for emergency use. We leave a thank-you note and settle into the bunks for the night. I sleep in front of the fire and chorus out my good-night to the other two.

After a wonderful night we awake to rain once again. It is the first of July to-day and George and I have been going for four months, and it's to-day we head for the most northerly part of our journey, and we also have to say goodbye to Duncan. The road bends and winds its way around the heather hills, it is reasonably flat on this track which makes it easier for Duncan who has to push his bike all the way. We round a corner and see a huge white lighthouse in front of us. We have made it. We stop to chat to a few people who are wandering about, having been brought out earlier by a mini-bus. The wind is gentle and as yet no sign of the promised rain. We all sit and admire the splendid view, out to sea as far as you can see.

George and Duncan are a bit low, to-day, for this is the day they part. Duncan has achieved what he said he would do and that is to walk with George to Cape Wrath, and he must now head home. I try and give him all my love, and kiss him gently, I know George will miss him dreadfully, he was such wonderful company. Soon Duncan gets on his bike and rides off eastwards, while George and I turn our noses to walk south.

CHAPTER 12

Cape Wrath to Shieldaig

Back across the ferry this morning, and then George and I are on the road to Rhiconich. George and I feel very lonely this morning, and when a lady offers George a hot drink inside her cottage, we welcome the idea of a chat and a bit of company. Presently we meet her three little girls and her husband who is a shepherd. He has two sheepdogs, Meg and Roy, who are quite friendly towards me. After many photographs we say our goodbyes and walk the road again. George and I head up a long mountainside road which stretches up and up, even I get tired, leave alone George. The rain starts again as we reach the top, the scenery is really spectacular from here, we drop down into a valley. George spots a man cutting Peat, we stop for a while and he tells us we are both in the newspaper, and shows us pictures.

We find an empty barn for the night, and next day, surprise, surprise, its raining. I found something dead to roll in in the shed and when George woke up he said I smelt terrible. I can't understand why George doesn't want me to love him this morning, as I usually do. George gets into his wet weather gear, and we set off at quite a brisk pace, the valleys and hills look splendid in the rain. The ground about us is covered in foxgloves and ferns. George says it is like walking through a beautiful garden.

A couple stop their car and ask George if I belonged to him. George said Yes, definitely, I was pleased about this as I rather thought they were looking for a dog. They invited us both to spend the night with them. They gave George directions of how to get there, and then drove off to make preparations.

We pass over the Laxford road bridge, and then proceed along the shore of Loch Laxford and soon arrive at Scourie. We pass a phone box and George calls Mum. Eventually we arrive at the caravan which belongs to our couple from the car. After many more cups of tea, with a great deal of fuss made of me, we eventually get organized for the night. I stay close by George all night, in case I was loved too much by the other couple. George did not appreciate this as he said I still smell of something dead.

In the morning we leave the caravan and have breakfast with the family in the house. George got a donation for the A.R.C. from Mr & Mrs McNeill, we all thanked them, me shaking a paw with them and we head off for the village shop to stock up.

We make our way to the ferry to cross to Newton. Duncan has caught us up on his bike as he has decided to go down the west coast to his home. He walks a little way with us and then rides off to try and find shelter for the night. Duncan decides to stay with us a little longer, so on top of the next hill, having found nothing suitable for us for the night we decide to turn right and go down a very pretty road towards Drumbeg. Duncan goes ahead again, so George and I enjoy the scenery, the rain having stopped for a while.

We meet up with Duncan at the top of the next hill. He has found an old landrover which will give us cover for the night. We all get in gratefully. I look around and find that one wheel is missing so no-one will take us away in the night. It overlooks a loch and is among very pretty trees so we feel safe.

After cups of tea, Duncan climbs into the front of the vehicle and leaves the back to George and I. He points out three great big red deer with full sets of antlers, down by the loch. I'm quite happy to stay where I am, these creatures have horns again, but Duncan and George say they are magnificent.

We awake after another comfortable night, but Duncan said he didn't sleep at all. Breakfast for me, and Duncan and George use the last of the gas for a cup of tea. Duncan has decided to definitely leave us today, and he will go via Ullapool as he is running low on cash, and he must get to a bank. Again we say we will miss him, his company and his humour has kept George going. We all part at 9.15 am. and George and I head southwards again. George and I climb up the various hills, crossing small streams and seeing massive mountains in the distance. George points out to sea, where we see lots of little islands, very pretty. We have now been walking for 128 days. I wonder if George intends to be home for Christmas? The day is warm and dry although rain is forecast later. We set off early to get the best out of the day. We head towards Lochinver. The sun is really hot and the midges come out. I snap and eat several, but they don't taste nice. We call at the local store and Post Office and then on to Inverkirkaig. We pass through and see a couple of people fishing and then we see a tent like Duncan had, and then a voice calls out. It is Duncan, it is 11 am and he is still in bed. It was good to see him again. He got to Ullapool yesterday but was unable to get any money so he decided he would come back and stay with us for a while. George is pleased. We pack his gear and we all set off again, consuming large amounts of water as the day is so hot. We re-fill from cool, clear, mountain streams. Duncan points out a huge dragonfly sitting on a flower in the hedge, I approach it but it flies off. Passing Inverpolly my foot feels sore, as I was limping George lifted it up and had a look at it. Apparently I have cut it somewhere, George wraps his hanky around it and it is easier, we head on

towards Drumrunie. We reach the 'T' junction in the
road and turn right, it is near here that Robert and
Lorraine Shaw from Lancashire, live. Meeting them
again is lovely, Cups of tea all round and then a
caravan is offered to George and Duncan for the night.
A lovely spot overlooking all the various islands.
After talking the hind legs off the donkey, tea and
meals,we are all ready for bed. We all have a good
bath before retiring, including me. Tomorrow we head
for Ullapool which is only a couple of miles away.

This morning it looks as though it is going to be
another warm day. George looks at my foot, I tell him
it doesn't hurt that much, especially as it had a good
bathe last night. We had breakfast and we are ready
for the day ahead. We set off for Ardcharnich, we
stop for a few provisions and then as we have a long
walk before us we set out at a good pace. We follow a
track which is not too good, then it peters out and we
are lost. The maps don't seem to show us anywhere
that we can recognize. We try and keep the sea in
view, but the ground is very bad and quite marshy in
parts. I get a bit panicky when George disappears
into marsh up to his knees. I keep close to him, but
George says he wonders what would happen if he broke a
leg or something. I dare not think about it, and wish
we had a nice firm road under our feet.

George and I climb up and down mountains and we dont
see any sign of civilization until about 4.30pm. We
don't know where Duncan is as he was on the road with
his bike. I do wish we hadn't taken this short cut.
We look over the final ridge we come to and see what
we presume is Ullapool. We are glad of the good
breakfast we had before starting off.

We set off down the mountain, I see a young deer, but
I'm too whacked to chase it. George falls over twice
but picks himself up again. We wade over a river at

the bottom, I'm not too keen on water, but I must stay with George. A couple out walking give us directions to Ullapool, we have gone a long round-a-bout way. George is very tired and as rain is not forecast decides to sleep in the open in his bag. There is no sign of Duncan, I wonder where he is?

Next day we are troubled by these horrible midges, my foot is also hurting, but we limp our way into Ullapool. George says his left wrist is hurting, probably from one of his falls yesterday.

At Ullapool we buy provisions and George finds a cafe for a mug of tea. We then set off to walk the whole length of Loch Broom. We eventually stop for the night and put the tent up, not to keep the rain off but the midges. It is a beautiful spot where the tent is pitched and you can see for miles. Loch Broom looks like a silver strip in the setting sun.

We have a peaceful though hot night inside the tent, but better than fighting the midges outside. We pack the tent up at 6.30 the next morning. The day is lovely so we really must get going.

We go to the stream to stock up before we leave and I decide to jump a fence. I didn't make it and got caught at the top. George tried to help me but I was in so much pain that I bit him on both hands until he got me free. There was blood everywhere which I was very sorry about, but I was fighting for my life as it were. We are both in a sorry state now. George says we must both get advice from our own doctors when we reach the next stop. His doctor and my doggy doctor.

We head on down this moorland road, George's right hand is still bleeding badly I try to lick it for him and say how sorry I am. George wraps a piece of rag around it and hangs it inside his jacket for a sling, but he is in quite a bit of pain. This road is so isolated but we eventually get offered a lift by a blue van. George says what we are doing and refuses the lift, but the driver Fred Stewart, is worried about George's hand. He says The Hotel Dundonnell is about ten miles away, he will drive on and make arrangements for medical help for when we get there.

We eventually arrive. The receptionist is very kind and has already located the District Nurse and also the doctor at Ullapool, meanwhile a cup of tea is in order and we have been told we have covered fourteen miles to-day.

We take a rest in the hotel lounge and the receptionist brings George a bowl of soup. We wait, and I get my wounds looked at by the receptionist and then I go to sleep. The doctor arrives, cleans George up and puts him on a course of penicillin. We thank everyone for their trouble and after George has taken some tablets and with his hand bandaged we are on the road again, looking for a place to sleep. On our way to Badcaul we spot a shed in the middle of a field, we find a few bullocks are in residence so we leave them to it. We see another shed at the bottom of the field so we make our way to it. Soon we are both settled, it's handy with a little stream nearby flowing into Little Loch Broom. George says he has a headache, so we dont bother with supper, we are both full anyway.

We awake next morning after a good night, but George's hand is still badly swollen. It is also painful, but all the bleeding seems to have stopped. We pack up our gear and head across the field to the coastal road again. It is Sunday morning, and everything is very peaceful and quiet.
George finds a ten day old newspaper in the hedge so he settles down to have a read while I snooze in the sun. We meet up with a nice couple who are

picnicking. They offer George a cup of tea which is
not refused. He gets a second one as well before we
say our goodbyes. We see people swimming in the next
bay, it looks really summerish. Another couple who we
had met in Aberdeen, stopped their car to wish us
well. They gave George a beer, and as it was so hot
he drank it. I tried to remind him he was on those
pills, and I just hoped he would get away with it. He
had a good long chat for about an hour and then after
two more cups of tea we were off again.

Towards Londubh, we pass a huge water tower which is
unlocked. A cool breeze blows through the glassless
window. George sits down to write his notes when two
men arrive to see who we are. George explains to them
and they say its alright to sleep here, so George and
I settle for the night. We settle about 9 pm, George
says his hands feel better, but they are still
swollen.

We set off early this morning as George wants to get
to Poolewe to try and phone Mum. The swelling has
started to go down in George's hands, so I feel a
little better. The cool morning breeze is refreshing
as we walk the two miles to the phone box. All is
well at home so we both set off for Gairloch.

We meet two very interesting hitch-hikers. They are
touring Scotland and have come from Leicester, hoping
to reach Skye to-day. We all sit in the hedge and
chat for a while. Eventually a truck pulls up and
offers them a lift so we say our goodbyes.

We turn right to follow a sign that says Red Point.
This is a very pretty narrow track with passing
places. Wonderful scenery as always. A lady driving a
car passes and then stops. She lets two dogs out from
the back, and then comes over to talk to me. George
sees a small boat coming across the loch towards us,

the lady says it is her husband. They are on holiday from Kent, and she has come to meet him from a fishing trip. George and I get introduced. This gentleman turns out to be a doctor, and he has a quick surgery there in the hedge. He looks at Georges hands and puts some cream on them. He gives him a nice cool drink and I share some of the water he has for his dogs. George tells him he is feeling very low. (I have noticed this for a couple of days now.) He says we seem to walk miles in this part of Scotland, getting nowhere.

I think George feels like giving up, and asks where the next big town is. The doctor says it is the pills that are making George feel like this and it will pass. I do hope so. He asks how many more he has to take and George tells him. He then gives him two more to take to-night. I lay on my back and the kindly doctor does a quick check on my tummy, but all is well there. He re-bandages my toe with a clean bandage and some cream, and that really feels wonderful now. We all have cups of tea from a thermos, and George and the couple talk for what seems hours. I fall asleep in the hot sunshine, and only awake when George calls. He says they have both done him a power of good with their chatter and help. We all wave goodbye, and they wish us well and tells George HE CAN DO IT. I know he can but I do wish the road would straighten out a bit.

George says we have done very well to-day, in spite of the many stops, and the doctors talk has really made him feel alive again. I am so pleased, I wouldn't like him to drop dead beside me. I think I would catch the next train home to Mum. We walk for another one and a half hours when eventually we pass an old abandoned house, overlooking Loch Torridon. George says we have both done enough for to-day and we will stop for the night.
The midges woke us up again the next morning so we

make an early start, taking the path towards Diabaig, and pass through a very pretty little village. We climb a steep hill on our way to Torridon, at the top we meet a farmers wife, who is also the district nurse. She has a quick look at Georges hand, re-bathes and bandages it and says everything looks fine. She checks my tummy and I get a dog biscuit, then she warns George of sheep movement just ahead.

We pass a camp site when we are hailed by a little family from the Channel Islands. I lay in the shade of the caravan which belongs to the Rev. Kyle, and then play with his dog Sheba. Mrs Kyle invites us to call at her home in Kilmacolm when we reach that far. George says he will, it is about four hundred miles away, but something to look forward to. George's moral is given a good boost to-day with the talks and the attention. He says four hundred miles is not far.

Refreshed, George and I move on our way and continue with our walk. We pass an information bureau where the lady tells us the ferries are running to the Isle of Skye, which is good news to George, but not me. We seem to cause a lot of interest around the bureau, and several people come over to us to wish us well. We then head for Shieldaig. A girl cyclist stops her bike and asks George if he is who she thinks he is. George says who does she think she has met. All in all we have a nice little halt with a lot of chatter.

George and I finish the hill, and set off along the seven miles to Shieldaig. Seeing a nice bit of grass overlooking the loch, George pitches the tent. We enjoy our supper looking at the water and I decide I'd like to sleep outside to-night in the long grass. George says not to wander away, and not to gather up any sheep in the night. I promise to be good, and we both drop off in a healthy sleep for the night.

CHAPTER 13

Shieldaig to Inveraray

We wake next morning and find we have had company in the night. Richard has pitched his tent next door. He has water boiling on his little stove and we are invited to breakfast and a chat. A Mr. Vickers walks over from his nearby caravan for a chat. Richard is a Geologist and explains to George about the formation of various rocks. To me they are just rocks. You go up one side and down the other if you cant avoid them. After breakfast George and I walk into the village. There is something very pleasant here says George, so we decide to stay for a second night. I get two bones given to me and we have long chats with the village people, George stocks up and then we go back to re-erect the tent at our camp site.

Richard and George chat away over more mugs of tea, while I sit in the shade of some bushes and eventually drop off to sleep. I am glad we are not walking to-day, I can do with a bit of a rest. Later in the day the men are joined by John from Plymouth, he is also a Geologist, up here on a project, everyone gets on very well. Later Richard cooks a lovely meal of corned beef, beans and new potatoes, followed by fruit and tinned milk, and then a cup of tea. I am allowed tit-bits and I lick all the plates clean so they don't have to wash up. The three men talk all night over a can of beer each and eventually get into their respective tents about 10 pm.

We awake early and get up, George says we must press onwards to-day after a lovely rest day. We call our goodbyes to sleeping bodies, who mumble a reply, and then we head for Kenmore. Richard runs after us and says he will walk with us for a few miles, before

returning to the site. George is pleased. We say our
goodbyes as we pass through the village of Shieldaig,
to all the friends we made yesterday. George says he
wouldn't mind living here, it is a lovely place.

Richard and George chat away, and he shows George all
the various rock formations and how they are formed.
It is all beyond me and I think George is a little
puzzled as well. We all stride out going a good pace,
and I am pleased to chase ahead. All my sore parts
seem to have healed and George is talking about taking
his bandage off.

We eventually arrive at Fernmore. This is the point
where Richard turns back. He takes a picture of us
both, wishes us good luck and then once more we are on
our own again.

George and I start the long walk to Applecross,
turning a corner we find two men sitting on their van.
They have a dog 'Rusty' who speaks to me. George is
offered a cup of tea, so that was that for the next
hour. Rusty and I sit in the shade and have a quiet
chat. We're invited to climb into their van where I
get a nice bowl of dog food and George is supplied
with soup. Rusty says she has had her feed anyway,
for me to go ahead and eat up, which I was glad to do.
They are on holiday from Edinburgh and come this way
when they can, to be away from all the crowds.

They both walk with George and I for a mile or so and
then return to their van. We look across the Sound of
Raasay to The Isle of Skye in the far distance. The
sun goes out and the drizzle starts. I suppose the
summer is over. I am starting to limp again, only
this time it is my left leg, and when George feels it
it seems rather tender. We slow down our pace for a
while to make it easier for me. The road does not
bend around so much now, and we are able to walk

straight, keeping close to the sea. We carry on walking south until we come to a sandy beach which overlooks Skye. George gets the tent up, and then he goes for a quick swim in the sea as the sun is out once more. I am happy to sit and guard the tent until he returns. I will have to see if I feel like it tomorrow morning, before we leave the area...

I wake up at 3 am and listen to the wind and rain on the tent. So much for the fine weather then. George is worried that the tent pegs wont hold, as the ground wasn't very good to hold them, but everything seems O.K. We get up at 7 am to a misty drizzle. We feed and then pack our gear. My leg is very painful this morning and I mention this to George. He says we will find a doggy doctor to look at me, and then we start slowly off, south again. After Applecross we climb up a 'forever' hill, the mist and drizzle are still with us and George says the road gives off an impression of the way to heaven. I hope not, I have a lot of things to do first. We climb up through the low cloud to find yet another hill just around the corner. We come across a small herd of deer, a stag and three hinds. We pass them peacefully, and my leg feels a little better for the climb. I am able to use it on the downward run too, so perhaps its not too serious. George is pleased too. Just as we are about to enter Lochcarron a Range Rover goes by and stops. It is Richard. George and he have a brief chat and then we see a sign for Lochalsh, 24 miles. George says he hopes we can make it by tomorrow as he intends to catch the ferry to walk around Skye. I offer to wait for him this side but he says No, I must come too.

We find a shed for to-night and intend to make an early start tomorrow. The sun shines and although I could sleep all day, George seems to want to get going. George says his hands are very much better, thanks to all the attention he has had, my leg still

hurts, however. We arrive at the ferry sooner than
George anticipated, so he is pleased. After getting a
re-fill for our water bottle we board the ferry. I
sit very still as the ferry rumbles across the stretch
of water and George is pleased. The engines do make a
bit of noise, but I don't shake like I used to.

We arrive at Kyleakin, on the Isle of Skye, a lady at
the Post Office there, gives me a drink of water which
is nice, after George tells her what we are doing. We
look for a cafe for George, we see one, but George
says he will leave it as the price is 25p. per. cup,
and that's too dear. As he says, he needs at least
four cups to get back to normal. We cross the road to
The Marine Hotel, the menu says A Pot of tea for 35p.
George says he can get four cups out of that, so in we
go. We then head out of the town to find a place to
sleep. The sun still shines and after covering a mile
we find a place to pitch our tent. I fancy sleeping
in the tent with George to-night, so as soon as he is
in his bedroll, I cuddle up to him and we are both
soon asleep.

We get started early this morning, while the rain
keeps away. George packs the tent and says he feels a
bit brighter this morning. The inner sound looks nice
and calm with just a ripple on the water. The wind
blows a little, but it is dry. We walk towards
Broadford, the traffic is non-existent at the moment,
we pass many newish looking houses and some young
forests. We pass a camp site as we get to Skulamus,
we head south and then George finds a lunch box in a
ditch filled with fruit cake and sandwiches, so I get
an extra breakfast, very nice too. The traffic begins
to build up and George nearly gets knocked down by a
large lorry, who comes so close that he gets clipped
by the wing mirror. I keep well out of the way, up
the hedge, I've had my session with a car.

George looks for a phone box to ring home. We call into a wool shop by the pier and a very friendly lady offers George a cup of tea. They both chat away while I sprawl away on a nice thick rug in the shop which is right by the doorway, and all the customers have to walk round me. I don't care, I'm tired. George tries to wake me by telling me about all the porpoises that are popping their heads up and down by the pier. I really can't be bothered, I would have to get wet to get them anyway, so I snooze off again with my head between my paws. George is offered a hot bath (I told him he smelt again, only yesterday), which he gratefully accepts. He sits in the bath and shaves while I watch, and then washes out a pair of smelly socks. He is enjoying himself as he said his last bath was at Wick. I'll look forward to sleeping with him again, to-night.

We leave our kind lady and find a shed for the night. It has a lot of holes in the roof and it has now started to rain quite hard. We climb through a hole in the wall to the next shed which is very dark, but dry. We sort ourselves out, have supper and bed ourselves down for the night.

Next morning, early we get up and make our way to the pier which is just a few hundred yards away. We call in to say our Goodbyes at the wool shop, and then we board the ferry. We pick up provisions from a local shop, I get a bone, the first one for ages. George says I must wait for it, but my mouth is drooling already. We head on, south, passing forests and hills all around, we pass through Morar and then on towards Arisaig. We stop for a chat with a lone hitch-hiker heading north, the way we have come.

The road runs by The Sound of Arisaig, we find an old boathouse by the sands. Although there are holes in the roof, George says it will do for the night. There

is a nice dry corner, and as we have walked twenty
miles to-day, we can do with a good rest although it
is only 4.30 pm. I am flaked out, I will have my bone
in the morning I tell George. We both have a very
good night in our half a shed, and next morning we
continue on south towards Ardmolich. The road is
absolutely beautiful, George says. I mistake a few
boulders in the distance for sheep and try to round
them up. George laughs, a nice sound which I haven't
heard lately, but then some real sheep arrive, and I
gather up quite a nice little flock until we come to
the next cattle grid where I have to leave them.
Stupid creatures they are, they should learn to cross
the grid, like me.

The road takes us up over a steep hillside and then
down the southside. George gets another re-fill from
a water stream, and we then both notice a small cross
mounted on a pile of stones by the roadside. This,
George says, is a reminder to us that we are not
alone, even though at times I feel we are. The rain
keeps away, and the conditions are ideal for walking.
We soon find ourselves passing along by Loch Moidart
and then into Ardmolich with its nice houses. I see a
salmon jump in the Loch, making a huge splash, I
wonder what salmon tastes like?

George says I am always thinking of my tummy.

We continue our walk through a pine forest. George
says the smell of pine is lovely. But bone and meat
smells are much better to me. We meet up with a girl
being pulled along on her bicycle by a large black
labrador called Bramble. He told me he didn't mind at
all as she gave him a good feed when he gets home.
Her mother is with her and she said she was a nurse
from Edinburgh. George chats away and puts the world
to rights, then we arrive at the little shop for
provisions. The kind lady buys me my meal for to-

night. We say our goodbyes and look for a place for sleeping. We soon find a grassy spot for our tent in some woodland, nice and private.

We pack up at dawn the next morning to get in a good day before the weather breaks again. We arrive at Strontian, and George stocks up. We find a very pleasant place to sit for a while, and then George fills up his water bottle from the Ladies Loo's. He didn't see the sign until he came out, much to the amusement of a lady passing by. We get tea in a cafe, and George manages to get four cups out of his pot again. It's amazing what little tit-bits there are under the tables. We pitch our tent for the night listening to the birds in the trees.

We set off early the next day along the banks of Loch Linnhe, we pass some kennels where the local hunt keep their hounds. I pass by quickly. they are making an awful din inside. George says there is grass growing in the middle of the road, this shows its lack of use. I can well believe it as we don't see another car for an hour and a half.
We come to an old iron railway bridge which we clamber across, this has saved us five miles on our journey, so we have done well to-day. Ledaig is only a few miles away and we must get provisions there before we look for our sleeping place for the night.

CHAPTER 14

Inverarary to Ayr

George is poorly all night. He doesn't get up this morning. I am not hungry so I don't worry about my breakfast, but George is only sipping drinks of water. Oh for a hot cup of tea, he says to me. I told him ages ago to buy a little stove like Duncan's, but he said it was too much to carry.

I wander out to the road to see if anyone is passing by. I could entice them in to get help for George. At least we have a roof over our heads in the boathouse. There isn't a soul in sight. George was right when he said going up and down each of these lochs is a wearying business. We should have nipped across the back of each one and it would have saved thousands of miles.

George has diarrhoea and sickness badly, he manages to get out in the open each time, but it takes a bit of doing. Eventually at 2 pm he says we must get going. He walks very slowly and after about 2 miles he puts the tent up. He tells me he has had it, I am rather glad not to be walking too much to-day, but I do wish someone would pass by.

Next morning George feels a little better, although not right. He says we must get on as we have run out of food. We make our way slowly to Cairndow. We find a tea shop for George to buy his cup of tea and this does him the world of good. It's on to Strachur. We stop briefly to chat to a farmer and his wife, bringing in their cows for milking. Seems to be a lot more cattle in this area than we have seen of late.

'On the road.'

After a few miles walking very slow we arrive in Dunoon. We stock up with provisions and boots for George. He finds a pair that will do fine. He tells the shop keeper he can keep the old ones. It is lovely now to walk beside George, I mean to say, I was nearer with my nose to his smelly old boots, than he was. We find a cup of tea place, and after chatting up the lady owner, George is given a pair of thicker socks as his are nearly worn out too. This has set him up a treat, and he really feels that much better. We head out of Dunoon to find a place for to-night.

Before leaving however we find the press office, the first report we have been able to make for over a month. A very nice girl reporter takes details and also takes the pictures. Then we are off again to find our camping spot.

It is the first of August, and we have been walking for 154 days. That's 154 times of getting out Georges bedroll, and putting it away again. Just did a quick sum in my head, I'm not just a pretty face you know.

On our way the next day we suddenly meet a man walking with his two sons. I seem to recognize him and then George says, "It's Fred from Devon." George had a drink with him at the start of this venture. He said he was coming up here on holiday and would look out for George. The two men gave each other a good handshake and a quick hug, and then we were all off back to Fred's van to meet his wife and family.

After about ten cups of tea and a hour later, whilst sitting in a comfy chair, George says we must get going again, so leaving our comfortable surroundings we once more stride it out. We walk beside the loch which is lovely, and watch for a few minutes as a large shoal of fish jump in and out of the water. We see a shed in the distance which on inspection looks

quite adequate for us for the night. There are some
houses nearby, George hopes we are not trespassing. A
lady however, comes over to see us. We explain what
we are doing and she says we can stay the night if
George will write her a little report for the local
newspaper, which of course he is happy to do. Then in
the far distance we hear the wail from a bagpipe. The
lady says it is a little girl who practices regularly
to the amusement and apparent irritation of the
surrounding householders. However George said he
thought she was quite good. We drop asleep with quite
musical tones coming to our ears.

Next day we are on the road once more when we see the
signboard for Tarbet and Helensburg. It takes quite a
lot of doing, going up and down these Lochs, without
actually getting anywhere. The most interesting part
was when we passed Loch Striven with its huge power
station. Masses of pipes stretched up over the hill,
and then we saw The Tarson Dam. Very impressive. Two
large eagle type birds take off from the side of the
water. Their wing span seems to be about 2'6" even I
am a bit wary of them and stay close by George.

George stops and chats to some road workmen along the
way. We share their tea, and with good wishes we set
off again. We find a tea shop in the next village,
which of course is impossible to pass by. On again
where we pass quite a variety of wildlife in the
water, including two sets of swans with cygnets, all
very graceful and peaceful looking. We stop several
times for a drink from the mountain stream, and George
fills his water bottle. The woods smell beautiful,
but there are a lot of black ants, huge things, so
George says we will press on before we stop for the
evening. I've never seen such big ants, and they
fascinate me, some of them seem to be about half an
inch long. I do however keep well out of their way.

We meet up with a school master with a group of boys from Taunton. We join them for a meal and then a good chat. Then after cheers from the boys they set off to climb one of the nearby peaks, whilst we keep to the lowroad. We stop at the next town when three girls approach us. One of them is from the Southampton Press Office, which we passed months ago. We all stop for cups of tea at a cafe, and an update of our adventure. I had to tear George away from all this glamour, which has cheered him up no end. Onward once more. We have travelled several miles in the past few days, but the weather is good and so is our progress.

I find a dead mink on the road. George says to leave it alone, it must have been hit by a car last night. I thought it smelt interesting, but did as I was told. The road twists and turns ahead of us as on we go, we head in and out of the next peninsular stopping off at Kilcreggan for a pot of tea at 'The Green Kettle.' George manages about six more cups as the owners are such friendly people. I get a bar of chocolate and a bowl of clean water. We chat to other customers in the cafe, who find George and I quite interesting. We set off eventually and stop next at Garelochhead for provisions. We spend to-night in the tent in a forest, I set into my two bones given to me by very friendly butchers The Kelly brothers, when we passed through Kilcreggan. We are soon settled for the night, and looking forward to a good rest.

Next morning I have another 'Go' at my bone while George packs up. We both have a good wash in a mountain stream. We are up to day 162 to-day. and it is the 9th of August. The sun is up and it looks like being a nice day. We round a corner when a long-legged thing is walking in the road, straight for us. I hide behind George, but he says it is only a grey heron. This thing then takes off and flies down to the waters edge to catch its breakfast. It's five

miles to Helensburg, so we step it out. We find the
local newspaper office and get a wonderful reception.
Photos etc: are taken, and then after a welcome bone
for me we head out of the town for Dumbarton. Having
rung home to Mum, first. We stop at a small stream
for George's re-fill routine, and then I lay down in
the water. George laughs and says to move over and he
could join me. Anyway its lovely and cool, and I feel
better for it. Near to Dumbarton we decide to call it
a day. We find an old brick shed and close down for
the night. Tomorrow we intend to start nice and early
as George hopes to reach Kilmacolm where the Rev. and
Mrs Kyle live.

The sun shines this morning as we set out. With a bit
of luck we shouldn't take long to reach Kilmacolm to-
day. I know George is so looking forward to meeting
up again with the Rev. and Mrs Kyle. We soon see in
the distance the Erskine Bridge. A wonderful piece of
engineering, George says. I don't seem to mind
crossing bridges so much lately, which pleases George.

We see a cyclist, flaked out in the hedge drinking a
mug of tea from a thermos. George licks his lips but
nothing doing. We pace onwards and then arrive at the
Rev. Kyle's. Cups of tea all round. A good hot bath
for all of us, and lots of chatter into the bargain.

George weighs himself on the bathroom scales and finds
he has lost two stones. He is horrified to see his
reflection in the mirror with all his ribs sticking
out, he says. His beer belly has gone, which I think
is an improvement. Mrs Kyle, takes all Georges
clothes and washes them I am pleased to see. She even
gives him a new pullover, as his is in rags.

There are loads and loads of letters awaiting us, and
George sits down to wade through them. He rings home,
and Mum says everything is fine in Devon. We all have

a good hot meal, and then as there are lots of people coming and going as there is a crusade in Port Glasgow, we are invited to spend the night with Rev.Kyle's friends, Martin Beattie and his wife Genette. I play around a bit with Sheba, the Rev's dog, I think we are both glad of each others company.

After a good night, George is invited the next day to accompany his friends to the Crusade. The Salvation Army Band are playing, and a really good sing-song was enjoyed by all. George said he didn't think he would enjoy it so much, but he really did. His feet are recovering slowly, but his voice is beginning to go. He is a little hoarse when he speaks to me. What with all the chatter and singing with so many people he is really in clover. We are invited to spend a couple of more nights in comfort, and George says we could both do with a rest, we have not had a bed or any comfort for over 28 days, not since leaving Shieldaig.

Next day, George is off to the crusade again, there are over 700 people at Port Glasgow, so he meets plenty of friends. Home again to lovely hot meals. Loads of food all absolutely delicious. George said he can't ever remember enjoying his food so much. Bed at 1 am, but Sheba and I have been asleep for hours.

Next is a baptism in the local river. George is very impressed, I had to sit on his feet hard, to stop him joining in the ceremony in the water.

After nearly a week of sheer pleasure, we decide that we really must get on again heading south. So with farewells to all and sundry we set off again along the road to Greenock. George did have a phone call from Andrew before we left. He is meeting us in Largs on Tuesday. George is looking forward to that.

He says he is happy to have met such a wonderful band
of people who are really genuine in their friendship,
and it gives him a lovely feeling of happiness inside.
I hope it lasts for the next hundred of miles or so,
it's so much nicer walking with a happy George.

We pass through Inverkip and stock up with provisions
and then head for Skelmorie. We look for a place for
the night which proves to be a derelict house, but
quite adequate and George says we will get up early
tomorrow and make headways for Largs, which is only
six miles away, but he is looking forward to meeting
up with Andrew again.

We soon cover the six miles the next day and we sit on
the pier watching all the tourists board the ferry
when Andrew arrives. He got away earlier than
expected, from his home in Glasgow, he said, because
his mother was talking about digging the garden.

The two men have quite a re-union, and then we all
look for a cafe for a cup of tea. While George was at
the Kyles, he got his tea by the pint, not the cup.
Anyway, he was back on normal rations now. Andrew
showed George some lovely photos, which he had taken
when we were back on the east coast. I looked quite
handsome in them. We are heading for Kilwinning, an
address George has from The Rev. Kyle.

Unfortunately we were hoping to meet up with The Rev.
gentleman, but he has gone to Canada on holiday. The
minister who did open the door to us gave us tea and
fruit cake, and let us use the garage to sleep in, so
we all have shelter this evening. We have supper in
the house, the minister is from the Nottingham area,
but it was good to sit on a chair, and chat about
Nottingham, and watch the news, before we made our way
to the garage for the night. We are awakened at 7.45
by the minister, who brings us a pot of tea and some

toast. This is very nice. I get a bone, and then Andrew sets off to catch the train home and to dig his Mum's garden, no doubt.

George and I say good-bye and then set off, passing through Irvine on towards Ayr. We set off along the coast road, with the island of Arran on our right. The sun shines and the sea is calm. I have a pain in my toe. George sits me down on the soft grass and has a look at my toes. I have a big thorn stuck in he says, he gently removes it and after I've licked it all is well again. We soon arrive at Troon.

George stocks up again in Prestwick, and then we walk on into Ayr. The drizzle starts again, so we decide to hurry through the built-up area to find a place for the night. We are up to day 170 to-day, and its the 18th. of August. Summer is slipping by. We find an old house again. George says he is glad of this as it looks like being a nasty night.

We go upstairs, and George clears an area of broken glass and we settle for the night. I am soon dead asleep and George says he feels tired too. Too many home comforts recently I think.

CHAPTER 15

Ayr to Gretna Green

The sun is shining to-day, after all the rain last night I thought everything would be flooded today. A boat sails by, up the Firth of Clyde. We have a wonderful view from the bedroom window.

We pack our things and we are on our way to Girvan and Ballantra. The rain comes quite hard, and then a cool breeze which dries us off. It's very nice walking along this road with the sea in view all the time. We pass a couple of ruined castles before arriving at Girvan. We pass a lovely white lighthouse on Ailsa Craig, it looks very inviting across the water.

The final six miles to Girvan are soon covered. We find the newspaper office, and George meets Tony Cooper. A very nice reporter who takes down our story, takes photos and gives George a cup of coffee. He goes to a lot of trouble on our behalf to contact The Rev. Foulds. This was another contact given to us by The Rev. Kyle. George calls at the shops for supplies for us, and manages to get another bone for me. Then we make headways for The Rev. Foulds. Before leaving the press office, Tony suggests that George and he go for a drink this evening. Of course George accepts this with open arms. The Editor and Tony, buy George a beer. I do hope he can walk straight afterwards, I wouldn't like to explain to The Rev. gentleman when we meet up what had happened.

On arrival we are welcomed in to the Foulds household with tea by the gallon, hot baths and a shave for George, and a welcome bed for the night. George says its good to feel civilized again.

Next morning, George says the night went too quickly. He does appreciate the luxury of a bed, a home, and good people. The sun shines, so after a very big breakfast for both of us, once more clean and decent we go on our way. We get on the coast road and head for Ballantrae and Stranraer. Several sailing boats are enjoying the water and I see a young spaniel dog on the beach. We have a quick play about before George calls to me.

We meet up with an American couple who make a great fuss of me, taking photographs etc:- Mainly of me, but some with George in.

George tells them what we are doing, and I then get a whole packet of biscuits to myself. He ought to do this more often I think.

We walk steadily on, George has a chat with a friendly postman, and then through a wooded area, which is lovely and cool. George says he will put the tent up as this would be a nice place to spend the night.

The next day, Number 173, the 20th of August, we can almost see Stranraer in the distance. We set off early on a sunny day, but presently hear the rumble of thunder. "Looks like a storm is brewing" George says.

We step it out as we pass Loch Ryan, the water looks calm, but away in the distance we see dark clouds forming. Two Irish ladies hail us from their cottage. I get a lovely bowl of clean water and George, his ever welcome cup of tea. They ring the newspaper office, who then ask us to call. It is here that George meets Mrs. Murphy and her daughter Helen. They give us food and drink while listening to our story. We leave our friends eventually and head around Loch Ryan to Portpatrick. We find a barn with hay bales. We make ready for the night, and I get the

juicy bone, Helen had got for me and we settle. The
storm outside breaks, its been threatening all day.
George says we have a roof over our head, so we drop
asleep eventually listening to the crash of the
thunder. I get a bit nervous of the lightning, but I
cuddle up tight to George, and he says it is all O.K.
Thunder and lightning won't kill us.

I don't feel too well this morning, and leave some of
my breakfast, I must have been too greedy yesterday,
what with my bone and biscuits. The sky is full of
clouds, but we set off passing a large herd of cows on
the way who were very interested in us. I didn't get
too close, as these creatures had horns again.

I see a very inviting garden, with the gate open, so I
stroll up the path. Geoff Sheppard greets me. He and
George then have a long conversation and finally
directs us on the right road to Portpatrick. I see a
huge caterpillar, all hairy walking across the road.
I have not seen anything like this before, so I decide
to follow at a safe distance, it suddenly turns
around, and I jump out of the way smartly, and get
behind George, not because I am frightened of course,
it just seemed the sensible thing to do. George meets
up with Robin Townley who is disabled, on holiday from
England. George sits in his car and chats for about
half an hour, while I sit under the hedge, out of the
sun. After exchange of addresses we all go our
separate ways. We are accompanied by the wail of
bagpipes, somewhere in the distance.

We pass by caravans and tents, and George re-fills his
water bottle from a campsite tap. We settle in a
forest for the night, very pleasant with not too many
flies about to worry us.

About 3 am I see something moving. I growl in my most
ferocious manner. George wakes up and shines his

torch. He cant see anything among the surrounding tall trees, but suddenly we hear a very loud roar. Enough to bring George out of his sleeping bag in double quick time. We hear more roars about 200 yds in front of us and then all is quiet. I hear a scramble in the bushes behind us. It's that creature again. I really let it know I mean business, and growl and bark as loud as I can. I will defend George to the last if I have to. A series of low growls goes on and then silence.

George and I eventually settle again in a very disturbed sleep. Half sitting and half lying, me with my ear cocked up high, and George with his torch held tightly in his hand, the only defence weapon he has. We are both glad to see the daylight, and really don't know to this day what the wild creature was.

We have nearly completed the peninsula and are now heading towards Glenluce, and then on towards Port William. I like the Luce sands, and have a great run around after stones which George is throwing for me. I run in and out of the water, and the whole world seems to be right again.

We have now completed the most southern part of Scotland, and Glenluce is in view. George says we must look around for our bed for the night.

The sea is choppy, and the rain comes on again, heavy. However, we have found a decent shelter for the night, and we spread out George's things to dry. Sky is still grey the next day, but no rain yet. We plod on towards Port William, and soon arrive. George could not use his radio to-day, as the batteries are flat, so we are not sure of the weather situation. Our first port of call was for batteries, and then we stock up with food. A little girl talks to George and asks what I am called. She pats my head and then

kisses me on my nose. Rather nice I thought. We then
start the ten mile walk to The Isle of Whithorn along
the A 747. The sun comes out and dries off the rest
of George's gear.
At a little cafe, George manages to get a bowl of soup
and six cups a tea inside him. We head on for
Garlieston which is seven miles away. George remarks
that the farmers are taking full advantage of to-days
good weather, and are busy harvesting their crops.

After a while passing through more villages, George
estimates that we have walked over twenty-two miles
to-day. Much too far, he says, so we look for a place
to stay. We see an old house with half of its roof
intact. We climb the fence and get nearer to
investigate. The house is ideal for us so we settle
by 6 pm to-night.

We start out at 8 am for Wigtown, George re-fills his
water carrier at a garage. The lady in charge makes a
fuss of me and gives me a very welcome cool drink.
George chats to three roadmen who are digging holes.
he also sees some huge blackberries along the road.
I wait patiently while he has a good feed. Several
people in Wigtown come out of their shops to wish us
both well. Apparently we are on the front page of
their newspaper to-day. One lady gives me a whole
packet of dog biscuits. We are made a big fuss of,
with offers of tea everywhere for George.

We are sorry to leave this happy little town, but we
must get on, we are now heading for Kirkcudbright.

After crossing the river Cree we make our way to
Creetown. Many heavy lorries rush by on this road and
I keep close to George. More forests along the way
shelter us from the sun. It has turned out to be a
hot day, after the recent inclement weather. We have
done quite well to-day, when George spots an old

woodshed in a disused quarry. We decide with the lovely view in front of us, to call it a day. Tomorrow, all being well we will reach Kirkcudbright.

George gives me a bone, and then I take a quick peep out of our shed to see several rabbits running about. I can't really be bothered. I am enjoying my bone, and I never catch any anyway.

Next day we pass through Gaterhouse of Fleet. George says the forecast is good, and at the moment the road is nice and quiet, so we make good headway. We pass Cardoness Castle, overlooking the Bay of Wigtown. We buy a few provisions and we are on our way again when Andrew Gray stops his car to offer George and I a lift. George explains what we are doing, and the two men have quite a talk. Andrew then offers George lunch at The Colly Palace Country House Hotel. Andrew promises to bring George back to the spot he picked him up from, and we all tumble into his car, me, thankfully, to drive up a long driveway to a magnificent hotel. I sit very still in the back seat with Andrews dog, who looks just like me only cleaner.

George enjoys a three course meal with Andrew, and he says this will set him up for a few more miles, I thought to myself, Days, if you ask me. My friend and I also get a nice meal with plenty of water to drink. George has a beer with Andrew. Andrew is a farmer and also a lecturer in Agriculture at a college nearby. He gives George a number to phone when he reaches Dumfries, to do with a contact at Annan. We are both very grateful to him, and then he drops us off at the point he picked us up.

Just opposite St. Mary's Isle we find a small derelict workshop by the wall. There is just enough room for us both inside. Tomorrow we make our way through Kirkcudbright.

The next day, day 180 and the 27th of August we get going early. A stray farm cat crosses our path and I give chase. It climbs right to the top of a telegraph pole and glowers down at me. I wonder if I could climb just a little way up, but George calls me off. I wonder if that cat ever came down, when I last looked around he was still up there.

We cross the bridge over the River Dee, George stops to chat to a man who read about us in last night's paper. He tells George he had spent quite a bit of time in Devon when he was in The Royal Marines. They shake hands, and he wishes us well and we are on our way on the 711. George stops to talk to four farmers getting their harvester ready for the day. He gets a water-refill with lumps of ice from a nearby cottage, lovely and cold he says, just right for a hot day. Apparently we were mentioned on the telly last night.

We head into the village when we come upon a small group of people. They have all seen us on the telly, and would like photos etc:- We talk for about twenty minutes. They had been out waiting for us since early morning, so that they could wish us well. What a good job we didn't cut any corners.

I was given a feed of milk and dog biscuits, which I couldn't finish and then we wave goodbye to the people of Dundrennan and follow the coast road for another four miles towards Auchencairn village. George stocks up again, when a lady in the shop asks George if he is, who she thinks he is. George says, Yes, and tells our story to date. We get a Fish and Chip lunch on the house, at the provision shop, and George crosses over the road to eat it in style at the house of Mr. and Mrs Patterson. The meal was followed by home-made scones, and as much tea as George could drink. George says this is lovely, and I lay out on the dining-room floor beside him. Apparently this good lady knew Mr.

Foulds, who we met over a week ago now. She then invites George and me to stay in her caravan in the back garden for the night. George says he would be happy to accept. He has a good bath and shave in the house, and then as we are both tired we turn in early. Before we did, however, Norman their son arrives, and he and George went down to the Smugglers Inn for a pint. I was happy to remain at home, getting a good rest. George soon joined me and crawled into bed, happy but tired out.

At breakfast the next day, George meets up with the Jones family, who are staying with the Pattersons on holiday. They give George an address in Aberystwyth when we get that far. So another contact for George to tuck under his belt.

We meet up with yet another Andrew, who lives at the guest house and is a farm worker. As it is Sunday we all go to the local Baptist church for morning service. After this is over George takes me for a walk around the village, we are joined by Mrs. Patterson's two grandchildren, Douglas and Lorraine. They show George and I a pretty walk which takes us by a stream, the children show us a swing they have in a forest, and much to my disgust George has a 'go.' I thought he might break it. I run about in the water and keep my feet firmly on the ground.

We return back to the house for lunch, and George rings home and has a good long chat with Mum. We all go to the evening open-air service, and I lay down on the grass among the children. I prove to be very popular, or so I thought, anyway.

We are both invited to stay another night, and then tomorrow we must be off again, we hope to reach over the border to England, all being well.

After a good breakfast for both of us this morning, George and I wave our good-byes, with so many thanks for the hospitality shown. George said he miscalculated the miles for to-day, and we will probably cross the border at the end of the week, not the end of the day. He was too tired to work it out last night.

George stops at the Post Office in Colvend for his stamps, two very nice ladies greet us. and give George a donation for A.R.C. Then we get two meat rolls, (very tasty), and a cup of tea for George. He repeats our story again, and I fall asleep on the floor in boredom. However I get a tin of meat given, and a whole tin of dog biscuits. We rest for an hour before continuing our walk and then it's 'goodbyes' all round and we are off south again.

We are about sixteen miles from Dumfries. We pass through a forest, when George spots a small barn in the distance. It seems to be in use with hay in the loft, and tools lying about. We will not touch anything, but we had better get up early in the morning to be away before we are discovered.

It is day 183 to-day, the last day but one of August. We awake early and George says he has thousands of tiny insects in his hair, I give myself a shake, and thousands of these creatures fall out. I sit down and have a good scratch, I roll in the long grass outside, and still they persist in staying with me. Will go for a swim later, perhaps that will drown them.
I have a drink from a small stream we are passing, and then we pass through the Salway forest.

A few miles further on Mr. McConnell, from the radio Salway stops his car. He gets out and we all do a' thing' for him walking around a field.

Mr. McConnell is a very nice chap, he would like to finish up the interview with a couple of barks from me. I am really not the barking type, and although I was coaxed and persuaded I really wasn't bothered. I mean look where barking got me in the first place. I hadn't forgotten that even if they had. Anyway they had all but given up on me when I saw a herd of cows approaching. Now, they had got horns, hadn't they, so I quickly said to George, "Come on, let's get out of this field." Mr McConnell was very pleased, he got his two barks to end the programme.

We heard the programme on George's radio afterwards, it sounded very good. You could hear me talk to the cows, and half of Scotland as well, George said.

When we reached Dumfries, George gets through to the local blacksmith, Roger Tresider, at Annan. We hope to meet him tomorrow. We call into the newspaper office where Elizabeth Martin invites George out to lunch at a local pub. Ian McConnell joins us, he wants to record part of the interview again so eventually we return to the studio. George is then offered the floor of the studio, for the both of us for the night. We are happy to accept. George is dined and wined again at the pub, and I am given a large bone. Lovely, we close down at 11 pm.

We awake at 5.30 am. George lets me out for a quick nip, the air is fresh and we are ready to start when Ian invites us to stop and watch the early morning programme go out, which includes us. Of course we are interested and spend a wonderful couple of hours absolutely fascinated by the intricacies of television, and the split timing of everything. George said he was surprised at the amount of work entailed to get a show out.

We pass some fishermen with their 'Haaf nets', these are huge mobile nets, with three prongs in the end, rarely used in England. They show George and me a salmon, weighing over 12 lbs, they have just caught. We watch a Cormorant dive under the water and bring out a silver fish. George says its surprising how long they stay under the water. We are told that this part of the country is steeped in the history of Robert Bruce. We head on towards Annan, when we get a call from Farmer Marstin. We are both given a great welcome, with cups of tea, and George is given the address of Mr. Marstin's son who lives at Helston in Cornwall, for a stop-off. They have all seen us on telly last night.

Half a mile further on the road a blue van pulls in, It is Roger, our blacksmith from Annan. George puts his pack in the back of the van among the many horse-shoes, and arranges to meet Roger later at his house. We meet up with his wife and son Mark. Unlimited food again, pots of tea, a drink at the local for George while I just stay by the fire and then bed at 12.30am.

After breakfast next day, George says it is misty for the first day in September, I mentioned that we have to expect it now, but George says he hopes to cross the border at Gretna to-day. We set off with more goodbyes, and so many thanks for all the feeding and sleeping etc.

We cross the border at 3.15pm. Hello England here I come I bark, we'll soon be home now says George, and you can sleep for a week then. We have been walking Scotland for 109 days and we are up to 185 days in all. Its the 2nd of September to-day, and we are just one day behind in our estimations.

After seeing a barn, we have our tea, and then we both turn in, our first night back in England.

CHAPTER 16

Gretna Green to Morecambe

We walk on the A 74 to Carlisle this morning. The forecast is for rain, so we are going to get on while we can. George says he wants to phone Devon today to say that he is now in England.

We go into Carlisle to the T.V. studios. Everyone is very nice. George has tea and toast, and then we meet the programme introducer, Eric Wallace. We go to the marshes at Burgh Sands to do a recording, which goes well until I take a bite out of the microphone, well I didn't know it was something important, did I? it could have produced horns at the last minute.

Afterwards we met Eric's wife and daughter, Sophie, who liked me, I could tell. We then head off to find Radio Cumbria, where we do a second recording, and then its the newspaper office. George did manage to get his phone call in, in between all this frivolity.

We head off at last for Burg Sands. The rain clouds pile up and as George has seen a barn handy we go in and decide to settle for the night. The wind is quite strong and the rain beats down on the roof. A family of house martins belt into the barn and then out again. I am busy crunching away on a couple of small bones, so they could have stayed if they didn't make too much noise.

Next day the wind still blows, but we set out with George wrapped up well. He says he can just about see the Isle of Man, over the water. He says he is surprised that it is that close. Maryport is just twelve miles away. Just out of the last village

George finds a phone box to phone home. While he is
chatting the rain comes, so I squash in with him. It
doesn't last too long and then once more we continue
our journey. The waves seem very rough as we walk
along, the wind is really whipping them up.

In Mawbray village we find an old corrugated shed
that will do us. George and I settle for the night
listening to the wind and rain. I climb on top of
George, I don't like the sound of the gale raging
outside and rattling our roof.

We didn't sleep much last night, so it's an early
start this morning. Soon we arrive at Maryport, and
make our way to the town centre and the newspaper
offices. Here we get a fantastic welcome, we meet
Iris Walton and tell our story, there is a very nice
atmosphere here, and everyone seems happy. We get a
bone for me from the local butcher, who also has his
photograph taken with us. Iris takes George for a
drink in the pub, and later we return to her home in
the town. George has a good bath and a shave and then
more photo's taken by a large boat in the harbour,
with a 74 yr. old Cornishman by the name of Amos
Trelaor. He has a lassie type dog called Trixie, the
dog has lived on the boat for two years, never
stepping on to land. He says it is the rule of the
land, and Trixie told me she doesn't mind as she is
well treated and has a good life at sea.

Amos told George that last night's gales did a lot of
damage. I'm not surprised, they kept me awake. He
wishes he was back in Cornwall. Later we return to
the house, and while Iris goes to cover a council
meeting, we have a good rest, and then take Bethany,
her little daughter up to the park to the swings.

We are invited to stay for the night in this lovely
warm house, which both George and I are very happy

about. George gets a new purse, which was made for him and also a new pair of trousers, his old ones were absolutely disgusting. We sleep well and have a good breakfast next day and then its off again towards Workington and White Haven. To-day is the 6th of September, day 190. George and I call into the news office for a final cup of coffee, then at 10.30 am we are on the road again. We plan to get within 2 miles of Workington before we stop. I lag behind George a little way and then a nice smell lures me into a house we are passing. I emerge again with half a pound of sausages hanging from my mouth. George is ever so cross, and we stride it out quickly to get away from the area. I am not prone to stealing, but I just couldn't resist the smell. I would like the owner to know that I am very, very sorry for what I did.

We pass through Wokington and on towards Whitehaven. Its near here that we have another contact, the Mitchell family. Soon we are at their farm, cups of tea and a nice welcome from everyone. I get a bone and large bowl of water. I am introduced to Mr Mitchell's many dogs, and I get a quick lesson in sheep dog training, the proper way, not how I do it, but I must admit I was quite successful on the Scottish moors.

George and I are glad we have made it this far, it is a lovely farm, and we have been invited to stay two nights to help us on our way. Tomorrow we will have a good rest day. George has a chance to reply to the many letters he found waiting for him, and I just sprawl out on the kitchen floor. I'm right where all the food is prepared. I'm not going to miss anything being on the spot. After dinner I watch out of the window while John rounds up some of his sheep with the help of three of his dogs. I consider joining them and showing how I did it, but then I thought it might not be wise. So I stayed and just watched. This

house is situated in a most lovely area, hills and
lakes all around, and we are right high up and can see
everything going on. Next day we must set off again
George says. After a great big breakfast we leave at
10.30, saying our farewells to John and Marg, and the
friendliness we have encountered. We leave Emmerdale
and wend our way south again. It is dry but cold.

A car pulls up and a man asks if we were the ones on
Telly last night. George is pleased that the
programme did go out, and assured the gentleman that
indeed we were the 'ones.'

George finds the post office to post off his mail from
yesterday, when we are asked by the lady to call over
to The Golden Fleece, public house, just opposite.
George and I did as we were bid, and had a fantastic
welcome. The landlord pulls George a good pint and
the conversation goes full belt all the time. Its a
job to get a kip with all this noise going on. George
gets another wonderful meal on the house, and after
thanking the Woodburn family we have more filming from
the news crew as we leave the pub. As the night is
getting on we must look for a place for the night. We
have only gone a few hundred yards when George
Woodburn and his wife catch us up by car, and suggest
we stay the night at the pub. Wonderful. George and
I clamber into the car and drive back. Tonight we are
out of the weather once again.

We wake at 7.30am, and after another fabulous
breakfast we say our good-byes to George and Sarah,
and once more head south for Seascale, and walk by the
huge Atomic Power Station. We soon reach the B 5344
and follow this for three miles which leads onto the
main road, the 595 again. Half a mile from the
crossroads a car pulls up and George meets Pamela
Clatworthy, a local school teacher. She saw us both

on T.V. last night, and as she just lives a few yards up the road she invites us in for a cup of tea.

Last night we again found a lovely dry barn. It is the 10th of September, and we have been walking for 194 days, to-day. We had a good sleep and the hay bales were comfortable. The day is dry, but probably the rain will come later.

We drop down into Broughton village, all is quiet, but George finds that he has torn the bag that carries his tent. He says we will have to try and find someone to repair it. We get a few provisions and then head out of the village to find our sleeping place to to-night.

We find another old shed and creep inside. The rain is coming really hard so we are glad of this shelter. Tomorrow we will head on towards Barrow-in-Furness.

We walk down the road beside Duddon Sands. George has told me to keep well away from these, as they are treacherous quicksands. I don't think it would be a very nice way to die with all my legs stuck, and then I wouldn't be the first dog to have covered this venture, so I obey George and stay by his side. We stop in Barrow for a cup of tea in a cafe, and scrambled eggs on toast for George. I get a bit of toast with a very small bit of egg. I suppose I must be grateful for small mercies. We set off again along the 5087 and along the coast overlooking Morecambe Bay. Here again the quicksands are notorious having claimed the life of a fisherman only weeks ago. It is along this road that George stops to speak to Mrs Peggy Raithbone, who is having a bring and buy sale in her front garden in aid of animal shelter. I inform her that I am in need of shelter, but she just pats my head and gives George a cup of tea. She phones the local radio station, and then contacts the Rev. Tipple at Ulverston, eight miles further up the road. We now set off to cover these miles, and wishing each other good luck we all part.

On arrival at Ulverston, we get directions to the civic hall where the Rev. gentleman is taking a service. We get there just in time for it finishing, but just in time for the start of cups of tea. George chatters to everyone, and I get a lot of petting by lots of children. They roll all over me and it is a lovely feeling.

The Rev. Tipple takes us home for supper and then offers us bed and breakfast. We are happy to accept, it has been a long walk to-day, George reckons we have done about twenty-one miles.

Awake next day to sunshine and the promise of a lovely day. We get on our way quickly to take full advantage. We make a quick re-trace of our steps to call at the village of Flookburgh. We have walked quite a bit to-day, when George spots a barn full of hay. We decide to settle for the night when the farmer arrives with a cow which has just given birth to her calf. He and George chat for a while, and then tells us to stay where we are and he will put the cow in a different shed. I go over close to the baby for a sniff, she can hardly stand on her feet, and I have to move back quickly when she totters.

Presently John Moore, the farmer, returns, he says George is welcome to come into the farmhouse to sleep and have supper. This suits George fine, I am asked to stay in a nearby shed with Nell, the farmers old dog. I don't quite understand but Nell assures me all is well. We cuddle down on a nice clean bed of straw, while George watches T.V. with the farmer.

We set off in rather dull looking weather the next morning. George remembers to collect me and then we say Goodbye to the farmer and his wife and make tracks for Flookburgh, we have arranged to meet Lowell Shepherd in the village square. He wants to take a video of George and me. Soon our friend arrives, accompanied by Arthur Phillips and Mary, all people George met at the crusade at Port Glasgow. George said it really was good to see them again. After cups of coffee we do the filming in a local field overlooking Morecambe Bay. I am getting quite good at being a filmstar now, and sit very still and stick up my ears, and speak when spoken to.

The film is really an interview for George on his religious beliefs, and why he is doing this walk. George says it was really good fun to make. We all have a nice pub lunch, and then after our goodbyes its south again towards Morecambe.

It is 2 pm when we pass through Grange over Sands, and we're joined by a little black dog. He accompanies us for many miles, and both George and I tell him to go home. He eventually spends the night with us in a railway shed, but when we wake up next morning he is gone, I do hope he found his own way home again.

A man pulls up in his van to wish us well, he has seen us on the T.V. He gives George a donation and then we look around for our nights stay. We see a shed in a field and we get inside just as the rain comes heavily. We are safe for another night, and will be dry. We are near to Bolton-le-Sands, and I soon settle down with a bone that George got for me from the local butcher in Carnforth, and then bedtime.

CHAPTER 17

Morecambe to Anglesay

We set off early this morning for Lancaster. It is a long road, but the weather is dry at the moment. On arrival we give our story in at the Press Office and then set off again. We have a quick look at the boats at Glasson dock and then on towards Cockerham. Again this is a beautiful part of the land, although the autumn is really upon us and I feel quite a chill in the air. We drop down on to the marshes, and the land is flat for as far as I can see. The rain comes on really hard, so George and I take shelter in a farm building for a little while.

We soon arrive at Pilling and then head for Fleetwood. When we ask for directions we are told of a short cut, past an old mill. George decides this is for us so we take the way, we pass The Old Ship restaurant and I go to have a look around the back. I find a lady in a red dress who makes a lot of fuss of me and introduces me to her children. George comes looking for me and ends up with a glass of ale 'on the house.' She is very interested in our story. We stay chatting for a while and then we are on our way to Presall.

Here, George calls for provisions at the village store and get a lovely welcome by the lady at the counter, George is given a cup of tea, and a dish of freshly made stew, just right for this weather he says. I meet Ben, a large black very good natured labrador, he told me he was also a stray at one time, but he had a very good home now, and he guarded the shop for his food. I also get a nice feed. Then we carry on our journey to find a sleeping place. George and I get a bit lost, which is becoming quite a habit of late. We meet up with Mrs Broadbent, who gives George more tea and a bit of chocolate cake. I think that George has done this walk on 'Cups of tea.' We then spot a pig sty. I am not too bothered about going in, they usually stink to high heaven, but George says its not too bad. No sign of any pigs, and its nice and large, so we both go in and settle for the night. George says we have done 21 miles to-day. We hope to cross the river Wyre tomorrow by the ferry at Knott End.

We wake up the next morning to a bit of sunshine. George says that to-day he feels like a bit of celebrating. I jig around the hut a bit, but he says that won't do. We are up to the 200th. day of our walk, and it is the 16th. of September. He will have to think of a way to celebrate our journey so far.

We slept well in our pigsty, but there is a great big pig outside waiting to come in this morning, so we make haste to get on our way. We say Thank You to the pig, who just grunts at us and we head for the ferry.

Eventually after chatting to many people along the way we come to Blackpool. I see the famous tower, but so many people are about, far too many for me and I am glad when George hurries along the seafront and reaches the other end. It has taken us the best part of the day, and we didn't even stop for a cup of tea.

We carry on along the sea front and come to a group of huts. One has a huge hole in the back which we manage to squeeze through. The wind is blowing a gale outside, and it has started to rain but we are dry and quite warm. So much for George's celebrations.

We had a good night, although the hut rocked a bit in the storm. We leave about 9 am, after a good lie-in. We turn our noses towards Lytham St. Anne's and Preston. We make our way beside the River Ribble. I enjoy racing about in the long grass, it is still morning and I don't feel worn out yet. Other dogs come to play with me and all in all we have a good time. We meet up with a group of people that don't look too happy at all. They thrust a collecting tin under George's nose as they are on a sponsored walk to Bolton. I tell them we are on a 7,000 mile walk, but they don't take any notice. I stop to chat to five children collecting conkers nearby, they are much more interesting. I get a big hug and a kiss from a little girl, which I enjoyed and then its out of Preston and head along the Southport road.

The rain comes and the sun goes in and we have only the sand dunes for cover, and they aren't much good. We pass through a wooded area and George spots a shed. Ideal for us, we get out George's bedroll, and he gets his wet things off. I give myself a good shake inside the shed, all over George, who shouts at me and we both have an early night. We hear a lot of gunfire, so George says it is a good job we are inside as there seems to be a lot of poachers about.

We are both awakened by a shriek at 2 am. George thinks it is a fox on the nearby railway line. There was a live wire in the middle as George had to carry me over to get to the shed, and the fox must have got a bit of an electric shock. Anyway all is quiet now.

Its fine this morning as we continue our walk to Liverpool. The road is wide and busy, but there is a good path so we make headway. We pass through several round-a-bouts, and eventually arrive at the home of Stan and Alma King.

We are now in Crosby and George and I are pleased to have shelter for the night. We receive a good welcome with cups of tea in a very nice house, and George and I stretch out, content with life at the moment. George says he can see the north west coat of Wales from the window, across the river Mersey. Our friends have a minah bird, which talks more than me and that's saying something, and a budgie called Buttercup, I am told it uses a lot of rude words when it gets going. I have a large bone all to myself, and George has a wonderful meal.

We are told about a ghost who lives in the house, a very old lady who used to live there. I didn't actually see anything, but I did have a funny feeling, but I felt it was a very friendly one, so I soon settled. George had a good bath and a shave, a good night in a proper bed and then next morning after a good breakfast, reluctantly we had to be on our way again towards Liverpool. Last night really set us up, and George feels he has had his celebration at last, although we are four days late as we are now up to day 204.

The last stop we had has been one of the nicest George said, this morning the sky is blue, so we are both feeling wonderful. We find the local press office and then are on our way once more. We go through the city centre of Liverpool. It is so busy, but we find the local newspaper offices and make our report. We enter a very large building by revolving doors. I have never seen these before, and I was quite frightened. George said he couldn't carry me as he had his pack on, but eventually he had to take his pack in first, and then come back for me. These things whopped you in the back if you didn't make haste and I for one didn't like them a bit. And then another thing I was new to, we had to go up a staircase that moved, actually moved, I ask you, give me the ones you have to walk up. After a lot of commotion George carried me, but I was certainly glad to get to the top. This experience was worse than the ferry, or the high bridges. We give our story and photos are taken, and then it's down a proper staircase and a proper door and out in the street again to continue southwards. We board the ferry and travel over to Birkenhead and then head for Wallasey, and pass the lighthouse there. The evening is pulling in so we decide to look for a shed. There is nothing anywhere until George spots a railway shed. We go in and make ourselves comfortable, the rain comes, so once more we have a dry night although we are near a busy railway line.

The next morning George is getting dressed when he lifts his right shoe a mouse jumps out. It gives us both a fright, and I am slow in the chase, however it gets away, George bangs his other shoe out well in case he had a friend to sleep overnight. We walk along the coast road when I find a friend to play with, I kick up a lot of sand when eventually we arrive at West Kirby. George stops at a little wayside cafe for a cup of tea. It's called 'The Quick Snack Cafe' which means nothing to George as he is sprawled out with tea and a lovely meal (on the house) in front of him. Mrs Davis, must have taken pity on him and thought he was absolutely starving. I mean, I was ashamed to be with him, he tucked into that meal so well, I got fed as well, I tried to eat more daintily, but in the end, I gobbled mine down too.

Much refreshed after more tea etc:- we are on our way again. We wave our goodbyes, and I give a thank you bark and then its on towards the border of Wales. We reach Queens Ferry as the rain comes,, having crossed the river Dee into Wales. We then head towards Flint, when George sees a small shack in a field. We cross over to it. It will do nicely for the night. An old man passes by and I go to bark at him, when George holds my mouth shut. If the shed belongs to him, he whispered, he might turn us out so I keep quiet.

There is a full moon to-night and an owl makes an awful racket from a nearby tree, I can just see him if

I open one eye. He turns his head right around, looks like its on a swivel. I cuddle up tight to George, as its colder to-night, but soon we are both asleep.

Next day George says the forecast sounds good on his radio, so we set off early, we have a contact in Mold, by the name of Martin Hallard but he is not at home. George assumes he must be at work, so we leave a note to say we will return later. We have a brief look around the town, pop into the newspaper office, the photographer goes to a lot of trouble to get both George and I right, and then on to the T.V. place, where the interest seems to be in making a film of us.

We return to Martins to find he has been back, seen our note, and left another for us to say he would be back at 6 pm. George and I wait. Soon Martin arrives. He cooks George and I a good meal. George has his feet under the table again. They have a lot of chatting to catch up on since they met a year ago. We all go to Martins local for a pint, and then its a good sound sleep for the night.

Next morning we are back at the T.V. studios for our film. It's the 5th T.V. interview we have had so far, so I know exactly what to do now, and then we are once more off, we have been invited to spend another night with Martin. We see ourselves on the telly, very good too except they got George's name wrong. Then its four more pints at The Leeswood Arms amidst lots of chatter and then after another good night, its off towards Prestatyn.

We are stopped by several people who saw us on the box last night, and wish us well. We stock up with food and head towards Flint. The tide is out and leaves a very narrow channel for boats with lots of sand on each side. We chat to a coachload of pensioners who have stopped for a rest. Everyone makes a fuss of me,

I even climb on board the coach to talk to everyone inside. They all saw us on the telly last night.

We arrive at Mostyn and George says he thinks we have had enough for the day. I agree, so although its only 4 pm we look around for a stopping place. We find an old shed that was once part of a Y.M.C.A. George looks around and tidies up a heap of old bottles. We settle down and call a halt. Tomorrow is day 209 and it will be the 25th of September so we are doing well.

Next day George stops to chat to a man putting a new roof on his house. He gets an early morning cup of tea and then its on towards Prestatyn only a couple of miles away. Entering the town George meets Ian Chamberlain on his push bike. The two men get chatting and then we are both invited to Ian's house for lunch with his parents. George and I are made very welcome, I play around with their two dogs while George is made at home. George tells his story and shows off all his maps and diaries. Everyone seems very impressed. We both have a splendid roast lunch, which George says has set him up for a few miles and then its back down the hill, towards Rhyl. We eventually make the seafront which is packed with holiday people, so George and I pass through very quickly to reach the other side.

George says his feet feel sore, which is unusual, especially as he has not walked so many miles of late, we now head off towards Towyn with its miles of caravan parks. We erect our tent in a grassy spot tonight. George and I seem particularly tired, I don't know why, we have only done our normal miles. We settle down looking at the orange lights of Rhyl, now six miles back.

We wake up to day 210, it is the 26th. of September and real wintery weather. George has a slight pain in his back, and on further investigation found that a very large spider had spent the night with him in his sleeping bag. He killed it and threw it out and said he never knew spiders could bite so hard. After all he doesn't let me share his sleeping bag, and I wouldn't bite him.

We head along the dual carriageway towards Colwyn Bay. George says his feet hurt, and mine aren't too special either. George stops to phone Tony, he arranges to meet him at the Toll Gate at Great Ormes head. He says he hopes to be there at 3.30pm. We hurry along quickly as we have a few miles yet to cover. The thick mist comes down however, and we can't see the sea now. On arrival at Colwyn Bay we quickly head through it towards Great Ormes Head, going through Llandudno George stops to chat to a man sitting in his car, and then to four dumb ladies. One of them tells the others by sign language what George and I are doing, so they must be deaf as well. I get a lot of pats from them, I feel very sorry that they cannot hear, because there are so many sounds to enjoy in this life.

On arrival we set off to walk around Great Ormes Head, as our friend hadn't arrived yet. George has a cup of coffee from a kiosk, and the lady gives me an ice cream in a cone, which I enjoy very much. I have to sit on my back legs and help her to hold the cone with my front paws. This tastes wonderful, I don't think I have tasted one before, all the people passing, laugh at me, but I don't care. We get given four doughnuts for our journey, which was very nice of her indeed. We stop at a pool on the sea front, and as it is still misty, George takes a chance and washes his socks. I behave as if I don't know him. However not many people about and no-one is interested in us.

We arrive back at the Toll Gate but still no sign of Tony. The mist is beginning to lift, and the sun shines over Colwyn Bay, while we wait, I get on with a bone, George has been given for me. At 4.30pm we decide to wait no longer and set off along the road to Bangor, we cross the river Conwy by a huge road bridge by the castle, we re-fill our water bottle when George says he hadn't had a bath or a shave for over a week. I should know this without being told, anyway at that precise moment Tony pulls up in his car. He had been unavoidably delayed. George is so pleased to see him, he has so much to tell him. He is going to walk with us for a few days with his little dog Minty. Now Minty and I had a lot to talk about too. I was also very pleased to see a friend.

We had a fish and chip supper to-night, then we all spent the night on a park bench under a tree. Next morning we find the car and Tony and Minty return the car to Bangor, where they live. They will then start to walk back towards us, and we will meet up again halfway. We find a shop for breakfast and then George and I set off for Bangor. George's feet are still sore he says, mainly the left one. We pass along the coast road which is very busy and narrow in places. On our right is the Menai Strait and the water is very calm to-day. The wind doesn't exist and the rain stays away so we make good progress. We walk through a tunnel in the hillside, which I don't think much of. When I barked it echoed round and round.

We pass through the small towns of Penmaemawr and Llanfairfechan and eventually meet Tony and Minty, we all walk into Bangor, stopping off at a roadside cafe for a cup of tea. The sun shines and we look forward to a nice day tomorrow, and of course lots of chatter.

Crossing the Menai Bridge we are to-day starting to walk around Anglesey. It is nice to have a friend beside me for a while. George enjoys his human company and never thinks of me being lonely too. So I am happy for a few miles now, and Minty is a good companion.

We follow the country road in the nice warm sunshine, it is so much nicer when the rain keeps away. Minty wants to run around and have a bit of a game, but then she hadn't been walking for thousands of miles, like me. Anyway she soon settles down and we amble along together, taking an interest in all around us.

A couple of horses pass us by on the road, Minty and I keep well in near the hedge. We stop for some food looking out over the Red Wharf Bay, which looks blue and calm. We rest up awhile before we set off again towards Brynteg, and look for Mr. Ray Milford's home, an address we were given by Mrs Davis of The Quick Snack Cafe, at West Kirby. We are given a nice welcome and of course, cups of tea, and then we are later put up in a caravan on the camp site run by The Milfords. It is a super site, and both Tony and George manage to get a hot shower, which I considered was most needed. A lovely meal and then a visit to The California Inn, and meet up with Bill and Barbara who run the place. Everyone is very friendly and chat to the men and make a fuss of us. Minty and me.

Back to the caravan for a good night's sleep. Next day we are away early after thanking the Milford's for their hospitality. They gave George and Tony three pints of goats milk before we left. Two of which were solidly frozen, and Tony put these in his rucksack, and one for drinking now which George put in his pocket. I nudged him once or twice with my nose, but he said I must wait. We head along the road and take a wrong turning, which takes us to a lovely little beach at Moelfre, but its a dead end. We go back to the turning again and find the right road to Penysarn.

I note that Tony is slowing down a bit. Apparently his feet are hurting now. He seems a little low, probably due to having to retrace our steps a bit to-day. Minty is O.K. and she and I keep going, until George shouts to us to come back. We stop in the village for fish and chips. We all sit on a grassy bank to share them, Tony gets out the frozen milk only to find the carton has broken, and all his clean clothes have been soaked. This does not help matters, so we all drink up the second carton of frozen milk, before that breaks as well.

We are seven miles from our target to-day, the sun still shines, so we get going while it is still warm. George moans about his feet again, I think the two men are wearing out. Mine and Minty's are O.K. We pass Point Lynas and eventually arrive at Amlwch Port, where we all stop for a rest, and then its on towards Cemaes. Tony spots a reasonable shed which will do for the night, but first we call in at the local pub for a pint. We stop at The Stag, where folk are very interested in us. The Landlady is super and invites us all to stay for the night. What wonderful words she says, and the men are only too happy to agree.

Both Tony and George inspect their feet. George's are really red raw and look very painful. They bathe them and George says he will wear two pairs of socks tomorrow, and look around for some new boots.

Minty and I slept below the open window and enjoyed the fresh air. Next morning the men woke up to an awful 'pong' in the room, which turned out to be George's feet. Minty and I knew where it was best to sleep last night. We go downstairs to a nice hot breakfast, and a good chat. Mr and Mrs Hughes who run the pub had taken part, or Mr. had, taken part in a round Britain canoe expedition, and was very interested in our little jaunt.

Next morning after breakfast we say good-bye to our new found friends and then we are off again.
The miles seem to take a lot of walking to cover today, possibly because we are going slower, however we pass LLanfechell and then on towards Holyhead. On the way we find a very nice little church and decide to make a night of it in the church porch. There is a good roof over us and plenty of room.

The next day, day 215, is the 1st of October, winter is really coming in fast now. It rained in the night but we were dry. On today to reach Holyhead, where Minty and Tony will leave us. They plan to catch the train back home from there. I shall be sorry to loose Minty, but they had planned to do this amount only from the start. When we reach Holyhead, we all have our last cup of tea together and then its goodbye to Minty and Tony and once more we are on our own again.

We pass along, the now lonely road towards the village of Llanfihangel where we stock up with provisions and then its onwards towards Aberffraw. The rain comes on but not too badly. The waves along the sea shore are beginning to get a bit rough. Several canoes are on the water, trying to ride out the waves.

We find an old bunker along the sea shore and George says this will do nicely for the evening. His feet feel better than they were, but my back leg is aching a bit. Anyway it will be nice to stop for the night. I have a bone that George was able to get for me at the last stop, but he couldn't get new shoes, so we will try at the next town for those. He has already worn out four pairs during this walk.

We find a dry shed, I open one eye and George is taking off his boots, so I guess that is it for today. I go to sleep proper, listening to the rain on the roof.

Chapter 18

Anglesey to Fishguard

Next morning we meet two little girls on the road who give me a big hug. They tell me to be careful about passing a house further down the road as there is a vicious dog who lives there, and he attacks everyone who passes by. This makes me a bit nervous, but we can't turn back. On reaching the house in question, the girls were right. A big black dog comes tearing out of the house, showing me his teeth. George just shouts at him, and I think its best to ignore him completely and we safely pass by.

The rain keeps off, but the sky looks black. We find the newspaper office in Caernarfon. We give in our story and have some photos taken by the castle and then its off again. George manages to get his new shoes in a local shop, we purchase supplies and then head out of the town. George then meets up with Sid Whiting and his friend. George is offered a cup of tea at Sid's house, which he says is really appreciated as he hadn't had a hot drink for two days. The men talked for nearly two hours, and then with food inside us we set off on the 487 again.

We pass Llandwrog village and keep walking beside the water towards Trwyn which is very pleasant. On the left are the Welsh Hills, where there seem to be plenty of sheep grazing. I could practice my art of sheep rounding-up, but George keeps on the road, so I follow him. We round a corner in the road when two pigs frighten the life out of me. They are close to the fence and as we come into view, they let out a huge HONK. George laughs, which was not very kind of him, but we progress onwards. We pass through

Clynnogfawr with its row of pretty stone cottages. George says that this village was his target for today so we will look around for a likely spot for the night. Further out of the village, George spots a shed almost by the water's edge, it is a very large shed, but we think it will be comfy here.

The next day George says his feet feel a lot better, and I seem to be O.K. so we pack up early to get on the road before too much traffic builds up. We stop in the next village for supplies and George phones home. It's G.W. phone home, not E.T. phone home.

George says we have two hours of walking yet, before we think of stopping for the night so we press on.

The coast road takes us through Edern village, up over the hill and then onto Rhos-y-llan. We find an old rusty shed but it will do us. We settle, when a little mouse crawls under the door. He sits on his hind legs looking at us for a while, and then climbs into a bale of straw nearby. I couldn't be bothered to chase him, so I let him be.

Next morning the sun shines, so we are soon on the go. We pass a pretty little church and cemetery, George remarks that everyone who is buried there is called Jones or Williams. As long as it is not Jack Williams I don't mind.

We carry on walking the coast road, on around the point of the peninsula and then head for Pwllheli. We are now on the A 499, with still a nice view of the sea. We look for ages but there doesn't seem anywhere to sleep, so we keep going eventually arriving at Llanbedrog village. We get caught by a flock of sheep who were being marched into the village by two men and four dogs. I was keen to give a hand, but George said 'No, to stay' so I had to do as I was told. Soon they went through farm gates and we had the road to ourselves again.

We find an old air raid shelter. It was a bit wet and muddy inside, but George covers the ground with an old sheet he found, lots of grass and straw and then his sleeping bag, and soon we are both fast asleep. It has been a long day.

We are up to day 220 to-day and it is the 6th of October. We did a lot of miles yesterday, and we were glad of a rest last night. We climb out of the shelter to a lovely blue sky and a wonderful view of the hills around. Lets hope the weather keeps fine, I do enjoy it when it is not raining.

On again passing over the first Toll Bridge to Minffordd, and then its the second Toll Bridge and from then on the road leads to Harlech. We seek shelter for the night as it looks like rain. We spot a shed and settle when a small boy with his dog sees us. He runs back to the house to tell his mother, who than comes to order us out. However, I lick her hand, George tells our story, her heart melts and we are allowed to spend an undisturbed night, in the shed. We are very grateful, as by this time it is pouring with rain. We awake at 6 am to the sound of heavy rain on the shed roof. I groan, its going to be another of those days. We pack up and set off across the wet field to the road, all the rivers we cross are brim full and running very fast. It must have rained all night long.

At last the sun comes out and attempts to dry us off a bit. Our next biggish place is Barmouth. We pass a young man trying to thumb a lift without much luck, George and he walk for a while chatting to each other, and then he gets lucky so we all wave cheerio.

Before crossing the viaduct at Barmouth Bay, we rest in the warm sunshine, and I have a short kip. The crossing takes a long time, and I keep looking down between the timbers of of the footbridge to the water miles below us. I don't feel too safe and try and nudge George along to go faster. Soon we are across and walk along the A 493. George says as the sun is still shining we will walk until 4pm before we seek shelter.

We find a shed in the corner of a field with hay on the floor inside. We make ourselves comfortable and hope no-one comes to disturb us in the night.

We awake at 7 am and George finds that I have managed to snuggle inside his sleeping bag with him, there wasn't much room, but it was cold outside. We get up and set off at 8am. It is not actually raining but it doesn't seem far away, but the winds are strong this morning. A slight drizzle comes but it soon blows over as we step through the town of Towyn smartly.
George stops to chat to a man who tells him all about his dogs. About life in general, and how little we really need to make us all happy, and then just before we arrive at Machynlleth the rain comes. We start to seek shelter. George wanted to cross the river to-day to reach the town for his cuppa, but we decide it is getting too wet, we must look around this side for a shelter. We find an old farm building, with a hay bailer, and lots of cart wheels. It is dry, so we decide to stay here if we can, and hope no-one finds us until morning.

We awake at dawn with the sound of the rain still pouring down. George gets into his wet weather gear, and I give my back a good shake in anticipation of what is to come, and then we set off again over the river. The forecast on George's little radio says its going to rain all day. Oh dear!! I'm glad my 'shaker' is alright and it still works.

We have just started the eighteen mile long walk to
Aberyswyth. The rain seems to have slowed down a bit,
and our progress is good. The road twists and turns
along the bank of the river until it disappears into a
forest. We meet some children, Jackie, Donna,
Dominic, Wayne and Mark, who really make a big fuss of
me. They tell George they will look after me while he
goes into a cafe for a cup of tea. George gets
talking to the owners of the cafe, then we all have
our photos taken before we are given directions over
the next few miles.

We wave goodbye and set off much refreshed. Me with a
long cool drink of clean water, and George with his
tea. We get coffee further along the road, by a lady
watching us trying to progress against the rain again.
We make our way towards Bow Village when a man gives
George more directions to the home of the Jones
family. This is up a steep hill among the trees. We
eventually reach the nice home of George's contact,
and receive a wonderful welcome. George gets some
home made wine, and then cups of tea. I have a little
disagreement with Hyde, one of the Joneses three dogs.
I get into trouble with George. We soon settle our
differences, and I am content to sleep it off while
George has a much needed hot bath and shave. George
and I are invited to stop for two nights which George
is very happy to accept. It is fifteen days ago that
he slept in a proper bed, 'and had a bath' I mention,
under my breath.

We have a nice meal and then we all go off to a party.
George takes part in a bit of country dancing, in his
hiking boots too. I made out I didn't know him. We go
home to a lovely warm bed after meeting so many new
friends. Next day we meet up with the local press and
the usual things happen, then after a nice lunch with
Mervyn at the Rugby Club, George and I are invited to

go to the little local school to meet all the children.

What a wonderful visit. George told all the kiddies about our walk. Oh the fussing and the tit-bits I got. I spent my time rolling on the floor with hundreds of kids rolling on top of me. Lovely, I thoroughly enjoyed myself and was sorry to leave.

After visiting the local pub that evening, with the headmaster we return to Mervyns home to talk until 4 am before bed. I was awake long before George the next morning. Dirty Stop-ups I thought, they ought to go to bed at a decent time, like me. Anyway they seemed to have thoroughly enjoyed themselves.

Reluctantly, next day, after a lovely breakfast we have to say our Goodbyes, and its on the road again.
We stock up with food and then passing along the road overlooking Cardigan Bay we arrive at New Quay. The time is 5 pm. There seems to be nowhere to shelter or even put up the tent, however we spot a bus shelter in a small hamlet so we go inside there. I go to sleep under the seat. George sees an old house up for sale, we find an outside loo that will just accommodate George and I. We must wait for it to get a bit darker before we take up residence.

After a cramped, although dry night we awake with the dawn. We both have a good stretch as it was only 5 by 4 ft but we were away from the weather. To-day we are heading for Cardigan. We were passing by some houses, when the 'Smell' takes me again. I go foraging and George is very annoyed when he sees me come out between two houses with a chunk of meat in my mouth. George says he does not know where I got it from. He puts the lead on me and we hurry away, with me clutching my prize. George says if this is how I'm going to behave he will have to think about giving me away. It's not as if I hadn't had my breakfast either. Anyway I hope he will soon forget about giving me away as I would rather be with him.

We make it to the local newspaper in Cardigan, after help from a load of schoolchildren, who all know about us from the news. Life seems to be very hectic here, loads of photos and reporters etc:- and then we go on our way towards Molygrove and Fishguard. A mile out of Cardigan we see a tin shed in a field. We settle in and I don't really want my supper. George says he is not surprised seeing that I had stolen that large piece of meat. He hoped that it would give me tummy ache. But it didn't.

Next day we set off towards Fishguard, but there are not many signposts around, and we have to guess the way a bit. We meet up with a lady, Alison Chandler who introduces me to her blind spaniel Lizy. She is very quiet an tells me its awful not being able to see. I feel quite sorry for her. We are invited back to the cottage for a cup of tea, where we meet Mr. Soots, her large black cat. As soon as he sees me he belts off and hides in a cupboard. I mean, I only wanted to chat to him, but he certainly didn't like me. Then we have to once more say our goodbyes and off we go on our way again.

On arrival at Fishguard, we do our reporting bit and then as evening is drawing in we start to look for a place to sleep. Sarah Rees is the local reporter, she also takes the photos, and then she offers us both shelter for the night. We meet John, her husband, and then we are invited to accompany them to a lovely old 15th. century house for a meal, cooked by Janet, another reporter at the office. I sleep on the floor with a golden labrador called Bell, while the humans talk. We are all very comfortable, and George has another real bed for the night

CHAPTER 19

Fishguard to Swansea

We slept well at Sarah and John's house and wake with the dawn, when George let Bell and me out. We chase next door's cat in our garden and then return for breakfast. Very refreshed we set off again, we are up to day 228 to-day and it is the 14th of October.

We climb the steep hill out of Goodwick, and wander around Strumble Head. The lighthouse looks out over the troubled waters as we pass by. The heavy rain comes again, and I have to shake myself more and more. About lunch time the weather improves and the sun actually tries to shine, as we make our way towards St. David's Head. There is a beautiful rainbow in the sky which comes right down to the sea.

As we approach St. David's there seems to be a lot of activity in the air. The planes seem very low and I creep behind George. I have never forgotten those planes up in Lincolnshire, when we were passing there.

To-day we head for Pembroke. We pass along the waters edge by St. Brides Bay, when George sees a small cafe. He talks about my nose, but as far as cups of tea are concerned, his nose is pretty good. We stop for a few supplies and a pot of tea, and sit and watch the waves pounding the shore below. We walk along the narrow coast road by Rickets Head. Not much traffic around at all. Just a post van passing. George throws a few pebbles for me on the beach, and I enjoy chasing them. All my feet feel fine again. The winds seem to get stronger, thank goodness they are behind us, but George says he does not remember such strong winds on this walk before. We drop down into Broad Haven and then as the wind, if possible, seems to get stronger we look for a place of shelter for the night. It is at St. Ishmael's near the oil refinery at Milford Haven, that George and I spot a pig sty.

Suddenly a hail storm hits us, and not minding the smell we both shoot inside. Someone is watching us from a house across the road, presently two little girls arrive with their father. We explain what we are doing and he says we can stay. He then returns later to invite us into the house for a cup of coffee. We then meet The Ferrier family and return later to our shed for the night. Mrs Ferrier gave us a pint of goats milk last night, so we enjoy that for breakfast, and soon we are on our way again. The wind still blows, but we were safe last night.

Tenby is eight miles away. George wants to see the press there, so he says we must get on. When we arrive we all get a good reception, with reporters and photographers in attendance. Heading out of the town we climb a long hill to Saundersfoot. George stops to speak to three workmen digging up the road. They give us a good lunch and pots of tea, and then its onwards towards Carmarthen.

We walk along the beach for about two miles, I really enjoy the beaches, they are lovely and soft to walk on, and I can pop in and out of the sea for a paddle if I want one. I have learnt from the early days of this walk that you can't drink sea water.

We pass through Amroth where George stops at the Post Office, and we also stock up with supplies. George is given a mug of cider to help him on his way, then up the hill to Pendine.

We stop at a little school where George meets the headmaster, Mr. Davis. George and I give a little talk to the children who ask many questions. We had been given this contact a long way back, but apparently we have got the wrong school. Anyway everyone enjoyed my company so we set off again after phone calls to the right school. We are greeted by the right headmaster a Mr. Thomas at the school further up the village. The school caretaker greets us and shows us to a little room. Mr Thomas and George have a cup of tea and chat for a while and then George tells our story again to about 70 children. Lots of questions follow and I get a lot of petting, which eventually I get fed up with. I am ready for a kip. As the evening draws on, about five of us go down to the local for a pint and a nice chat, and then its a return to the school for the night. A proper bed for George again.

We awoke at 7 am, and had a lovely breakfast, and then its a big school group picture with us all in before our departure. The sun is out and the forecast is good for the day. George has instructions to call on yet another school in the next village, which is only four miles away, so we get our gear together and set off. Laugharne lays along the coast road, the sea is sparkling in the sunshine this morning, when suddenly a car pulls in, it is the Head of the next school, a Mr. Rees. I leap into the back seat immediately, I try to tell George to get in too, but he says No, and for me to get out. George tells Mr. Rees he will walk to the school and get there about 11.45 in time for lunch. So while Mr. Rees goes ahead we plod along.

We all get a wonderful reception from the school children who give us three cheers. We all have a very nice lunch before our talk in the afternoon to the children. Loads of questions and then Mr. Rees phones a Mr. Harris the Headmaster of a school at St. Clears, who wants us to talk to his children. We are on to a good thing here, I say to George in my doggy way.

Plenty of food, plenty of tea and a warm bed at night. I hope it will last for a while yet.

We stop at the local butchers on the way and I get two bones, a cup of tea for George who is recognized and then we hurry along to our next stop. We pass a school bus on the way with a load of school children who are going swimming, they recognize us and all cheer out of the windows.

We arrive at Mr. Harris's house where we are given a lovely tea by Mrs. Harris, and then Mr. Harris, George and I go down to the Maenllwyd Inn, where we have an enjoyable evening, chatting away, in the meantime I have found a log fire to lay in front of. We then return to the school where we are able to stay for the night. Before George gets into his sleeping bag he looks through some of the school books, and as it is near to Halloween he reads some ghost stories. After a while he decides it is time to settle down. He puts out the lights, lays back in his bedroll when he sees a huge round face looking at him. He points it out to me and I growl. However on further investigation we find some big pumpkins, all gorged out to represent faces hanging on a string by the window. The full moon had come up and was shining right through them, giving a very weird impression. George says he is not going to read any more ghost stories for a while.

The next day is the 20th of October and we are up to day 234 in our walk. We slept well and the forecast is good so we get going as we have two more schools to talk to to-day. The first one is at Llanstephan and then its on to The Queen Elizabeth school at Carmarthen.

George takes me out for a leg stretch first thing. There is a touch of frost about after the summer. I have a feeling that our remaining miles are going to be jolly cold at night.

The children soon arrive at school and George and I get a good send off. They wave us all up the dual carriageway until we are out of sight. The road soon drops down into the village and George asks directions to the local school.

We both receive a nice welcome from Mr. Owen, the next headmaster. We do our 'Little talk' with questions of course. We both have a lovely lunch at the school, and I have found out that under the tables at these schools is like a fairyland. I get little hands with tit-bits waving to and fro, and I very gently take what is offered. I can hardly stand at the end of the meal. George says we must press on, but I would rather have slept off my big extra dinners.

After our good send off, George says to me he is developing a very soft spot for the Welsh people, everybody has been so kind to us since we crossed the border. I have lots of soft spots personally for anyone who offers me something to eat. George says I must stop being so greedy, but I notice that he enjoys his meals on a plate too.

We have seven miles to cover in two hours to reach The Queen Elizabeth school, so we must walk smartly. We make good time, despite the light rain that falls for most of the journey. We meet Mr. Stephens, the next Headmaster and give a short talk to the sixth formers. We answer a few questions before going home time.

Later George and I meet Mrs Williams in the school canteen, and we both get yet another splendid meal. George says he is going to miss all this when we have to return to a cold meal in a cold shed, and I agree. We could, I suggested to him stay on. He could keep talking and I would guard the school, but all good things will eventually end I am told. To-night at any rate we are safe. A bed is made up for George at the school, and I sleep on a rug beside him. Oh, the comfort of it.

I go out for a stroll at 7 am, and then Mr. Stephens calls to say breakfast is ready. George and I go along to the kitchen, where we get a good fry up by Mrs. Williams. We set off before school comes in after saying Goodbye to all the staff, and our many thanks. We head for Carmarthen, and I think to myself, 'That's it, then, no more schools on the schedule.' We are back to the nitty gritty. We cross the river and head down the other side towards Ferryside and Kidwelly.

We stock up with provisions and on top of the next hill, George says he can just see The Gower Peninsula, our target for tomorrow. We arrive at Pembrey, the R.A.F. are flying low, so George puts me on the lead. We find an old railway truck in a siding, and I am told we could sleep under this to-night. It is cold and I try and get into the sleeping bag once again, but George is still awake and throws me out. Oh, for a nice warm school.

The next day we set off briskly to warm ourselves up. We meet a early postman from whom George asks directions. We meet Margaret Phillips who is taking in her post. She invites us in for a cup of tea, and we both end up with a jolly good breakfast inside us. George meets Bernard, her husband, and I stretch out in front of a nice warm fire.

We head towards Llanelli, where George calls at the press office. This is closed as we find out it is Saturday, George says he has lost Friday, he grumbles about it missing from the week we have just had.

Western Mail and Echo.
Cardiff.
'A willing school guard.'

We keep going as George says we have to go around another little peninsula before passing Swansea, tomorrow, or the next day. We meet up with Mr. Howell and his son Christian who walk the last six miles with us. This is good company for us both. We cross some stepping stones after the sand dunes at Three Cliffs Bay. The tide was just lapping the top of them so we had to be quick, then up onto the golf course where I had a bit of a run-about before reaching Mrs. Smiths house. We get a good welcome from David and Pamela Clatworthy, who George met weeks ago in Cumberland. We have a nice tea and a shower before setting off to Swansea for a party. A nice time was had by all and then it was a warm bed again, in a house with a roof. It has just gone midnight.

We are away early next day, after a good breakfast for both of us. We hope to meet the Millard family as we pass through the next village of Bishopston, so we try to make an early start after saying our Thank-You's nicely. David walks with us part of the way and then returns home while we go on. We arrive to another warm welcome, with cups of tea galore, and later we have a pleasant walk along the Mumbles. We see the first signs of the Devon Coast and George points it out to me and says 'That is home, Jack' This is news to me, and it sounds wonderful. I had begun to wonder if there ever was a ' home' again.

Before leaving George is given another address to call on at Portishead, I am anxious to get on now that home has been mentioned. We have another good meal and George is invited to stay for yet another night before reaching Swansea tomorrow. We are only a couple of miles away so this will be nice.

CHAPTER 20

Swansea to Dunster

After breakfast this morning we are invited to stay yet another night. The idea being we could walk to Swansea today and go to the press office, and then down to the pier where Craig is fishing, with Misty the dog. His father will pick him up later in the day, and then he will bring us back the next day to the point where he picked us up. Sounds wonderful, George and I walk to the beach, and intend to walk the five miles to Swansea on the sea shore. I do enjoy this, we are away from the traffic, and it's more interesting with little crabs in the rock pools etc.

Eventually we reach the press offices, where stories and pictures are taken. George calls at the post office for stamps and then we make our way to the B.B.C. studios, where a great welcome awaits us. George says that perhaps I will now become famous as it is a world wide programme. He says he hopes so, because I am the first dog to have walked this far. Arrangements were made for the B.B.C. at Cardiff to phone the Millards house to make the arrangements for an appointment when we arrive that far, and so do another report.

We have to meet Craig at four o.clock at the pier, so after all this excitement we make our way there. We can just make out the North Devon coast from where we stand, and I think that George feels a bit homesick. I know I feel a lot homesick, so when our transport arrives we are quite pleased to all scramble in to go back for another night to a lovely house. Craig hadn't caught anything, but he doesn't seem to mind. Misty and I have a kip in the back of the car.

We awake next day to day 239 on our walk, it is the 25th of October and really wintery now. I wonder if we will be home for Christmas? The B.B.C. ring at 8.15am and George does a quick talk about our adventure. Arrangements are made to meet them in Cardiff when we arrive.

After a good breakfast once again, we get into the car to be dropped off at Swansea pier. A good start to our day. The point we had walked to, yesterday.

We say farewell to Misty, who I have got quite fond of these last few days, and then with pats and handshakes all round we are off again. We pass the quiet little village of Kenfig, when a van draws up and offers us a lift. George explains what we were doing, and the man said he knew, he was just testing us to see if we would cheat or not. I didn't think much of this, and was ready and willing if George had said to have a 'Go' at him. Anyhow we went on our way and left him to think it out.

It is getting on for 3.30pm, and George reminds us that the clocks went back a couple of nights ago, and it is really now 4.30pm. We ought to be looking for a place for the night. I couldn't agree more. We have done quite a few miles to-day. We walk through the village before Porthcawl, and after climbing a very steep hill, we all sit down for a rest.

We see a barn to stay out of the weather. A farmer sees us and is concerned about me chasing his sheep. George says we are both dead tired, and I'm on a chain anyway, so he agrees that we can stay. We settle in among the hay bales and have a comfortable night.

The next morning we are away early as it is quite frosty. Most of the leaves have fallen from the trees, and winter is truly setting in. We pass the

R.A.F. base at St. Athan's camp and soon arrive at
Rhoose village. There are lots of boats going up and
down the channel here, and the water seems quite busy.

The sun is shining, and the sky is blue, so we intend
to get going while the going is good. Three ladies
who have seen us on T.V. stop us to wish us well, and
then its on into Barry. We find the press offices,
and give in our story. The welcome is warm, and then
we head on along the coast. George spots the Somerset
coast line on the far shore, we are getting nearer to
our crossing point now.

On arrival at Penarth we seek the Phillips home, our
next contact. We get a good welcome cup of tea, and a
nice fire which I have found to sit by. We have a
lovely restful evening, with lots of information given
to us on the birdlife hereabouts by Mr. Philips, and
after a meal, a lovely bed for George again, and a rug
for me to sleep on. This is good, long may it last.

After breakfast we say goodbye to another nice family,
and head off towards Cardiff, which is four miles
away. The sun still shines as we stride it out. We
give our story in at Cardiff news office, and lots
more photos before we again set off to find the local
radio station, where we do yet another broadcast, and
George gets a glass full of coffee, as there seems to
be a cup shortage.

We have a quick look around the town, and George calls
into the local P.D.S.A. offices where I am given a
meal before we set off again. We are now heading for
Rumney where George hopes to see another of his
contacts. We are greeted with the famous welcome by
Mrs Herrick, cups of tea, a good meal and then George
and Mr. Herrick settle down to look at George's notes
and maps of what we have done to date. Mr. H. does a
good repair job on George's maps as they are falling

to pieces, he's opened and shut them so many times.
They talk for a long time, and then its bed again in a
nice warm house.

After breakfast the next day we thank Mrs Herrick for
looking after us and then its on the road once more,
we are hoping that we might reach the bridge to-day to
cross the river Severn to Somerset. Mr Herrick joins
us for a mile or two before turning back and then its
on towards Newport. The area is flat and the day is
good, so we cover quite a few miles before stopping
for a little rest. We head out of Newport along the
Chepstow road. We meet Adrian and Lindsey, while
Adrian is busy cutting his hedge. I walk in and
Lindsey makes a fuss of me. George is then invited in
for a cup of tea. They hear our story to date and we
are both invited to stay the night. This is extremely
kind of them, and after much more chatter and a good
meal we are suited again, with a roof over our heads.
George says we are very lucky as by now there is a
heavy frost outside. I know we are lucky, it was me
who made the first move, remember?

We awake after a good sleep, we are up to day 244 and
it is the day before the last in October. Soon be
bonfire night. We hope to cross the Severn Bridge to-
day. After a good breakfast, we stay talking again.
Lindsey invites us to stay for a second night and have
a good rest, and George, I am pleased to say, accepts.

We have a really good rest to-day. George goes with
Adrian to the local pub and we all meet Lindseys
parents and sister, who have come especially to see
us. The local radio are contacted so we will do
another recording at 7.45am tomorrow, before we set
off again.

We awake next morning to a little drizzle, but after
breakfast, Lindsey drives us down to the local radio

station where we do another interview which goes out live. We then return to the house where we get another good breakfast before we start out again. Tomorrow is the 1st of November, and boy, can you feel it in the air.

We thank Lindsey for all her kindnesses and after a last wave we go on our way. We pass through The Magor valley. Soon we arrive at The Severn Bridge and start crossing it in a light wind. The traffic however is very heavy by this time, and I am not too happy with it being so close. It is a long, long walk across, and I am more than happy to reach the other side. I was sick on the way over. The bridge quivered every time something heavy rumbled by, and it really frightened me, however I was O.K. as soon as we got on to firm ground again. I am sad however to leave Wales and our many new friends we have found.

On the other side we meet a Mr. Hatton and his son Nigel, who are sitting on the grass verge looking at all the traffic. We sit for a while and tell our story, then Mr. Hatton says if we would like he would give us a lift to Swindon, which is 30 miles away, to meet up with George's friend Dave. This was a long standing arrangement, made months ago, we had to ring Dave when we got over the bridge and he was going to pick us up. Then it was going to be a good rest for a few days, and he would return us to the bridge again. This offer would save Dave, half the journey. We gratefully accept, and I am into the driving cab before you can say Jack Robinson.

I sleep most of the way, while George eats Mr. Hattons sandwiches. We arrive eventually at the R.A.F. Hospital at Wroughton. We thank Mr. Hatton gratefully for the lift and we head off to find Dave, where we get a nice welcome once again. After a lovely restful few days we must be off again on the last phase of

our journey. Dave will drop us off at The Severn
Bridge tomorrow morning.

We awake to day 252, and it is the 7th of November.
We say Goodbye to Jackie, and we are dropped off at
our pick-up point on the end of the bridge, and then
we set our noses west. We are on our own again. Soon
the two towers of the bridge fade from view as we head
along the 3124 towards Avonmouth. The road is very
busy with large lorries, the paths are not good, but
we soon cover the miles. We try to look across the
water to Wales, but we cannot see as there is quite a
mist hanging about. We can only remember the memories
and friends that we made there.

Both George and I feel good to be heading westwards
before the winter finally arrives. We soon find
ourselves walking through the Industrial estate of
Avonmouth. We pass over the Avon Bridge, getting a
wonderful view of the countryside around. We now head
on towards Portishead where the Lewis family live,
people we met while George and I were in Swansea two
weeks ago. We get a nice welcome and later George
goes with Mr. Lewis to Bristol for a drink, while the
children go to a party. I stay at home, glad to have
a quiet rest. A good roof over our heads, and a bed
for George.

Next day after breakfast, we say our goodbyes and
thank yous. George says he seems to have caught a
cold over the last few days. He reckons it is all the
central heating we have enjoyed of late. I tell him
he can sleep in the outside shed in future, I at least
enjoyed the warmth of central heating.

We head for Clevedon, a distance of two miles, so
quickly we cover it, stopping at a little shop on the
way for supplies. The trees around are very pretty
although the leaves are falling fast. I have a roll

in the thick carpet of leaves, and kick my legs in the air. We have covered five miles when a car pulls up. George meets Mr. Davis, the headmaster of St. Peter's school in Portishead. He'd met Mrs Lewis who had told him about us. George is invited to return the last few miles to talk to the children. This he is quite happy to do, so we pile into his car and set off back to Portishead. We meet up with the children. George talks for 25 minutes. Lots of questions and a fuss for me, and then we talk to the infants. I liked this better because we can have a rough and tumble on the floor afterwards.

Mr Davis then said he'd rung Clevedon School, the headmaster being a Mr. Tom Riley, and would we talk to his children. George says he enjoys doing this, and of course we will. We are taken to Clevedon by car as of course we have already walked this far.

We both get a nice meal on the 'School' as it were, and after more talks and questions we set out once more. As it is just after lunch time, the newspaper office is still shut. We wait outside when an old lady comes along and asks George to sweep up the leaves on the path. He tells her he is sorry he hadn't got a brush. After all she thought he was a road sweeper he looked that scruffy, she goes on her way muttering to herself.

The newspaper office opens and we give in our stories. I lay on my back with my feet in the air, so that everyone can rub my tummy, which they do. After photos etc., and much interest, George is given two mugs of coffee and then its off once more.

We now look for the home of the Wike family. We have not covered many miles to-day, but George says the talks to the schools are more important. Mr Wike is a teacher at St. Peter's school and he invited us to

stay for tonight. We both get a good welcome, a
lovely hot meal, and another bed for the night. It is
lovely to live in civilized style. Tomorrow George is
invited to go to The Mary Elton school before we leave
the area for another talk.

I sleep all through the next talk, after all I've
heard it all before. I only awake when the applause
comes at the end. George gets a cup of coffee and
then we are on the road again. The ground is very
flat which makes for easier walking so we set up a
good pace. We follow the road over the M5 motorway
which goes through Yatton, and then its Weston-Super-
Mare. We report to the news office, and pictures are
taken of us on the sea front. George goes in search
of supplies and then we must look for a place to
sleep. George gets a cup of tea at a cafe, and then
we head out of the town. Its 6 pm now, and getting
quite dark. We see a field and George erects the tent
among many cow pats. I am warned not to go near them,
and to remember many months ago, when I did.

We did sleep well, although it is a far cry from a
real bed said George. We pack up and set off again
heading up the hill towards Burnham-on-sea. We meet a
nice farmer on the way who tells George it will not
rain to-day. We then, to my delight, walk along the
beach for about four miles. I chase in and out of the
water and run after stones, until I am quite worn out.

The newspaper office is at Highbridge, so we follow
the path along the riverbank from Burnham, and soon
arrive. However we are then told the Newspaper office
is in Burnham, so we decide to leave it as we are both
a bit tired by now. I get a bone given to me by the
local butcher which was kind of him, there doesn't
seem much cover, so it looks like its a tent job again
to-night.

We sleep well and we are up to day 256 to-day, and it is the 11th of November. We head back along the waterside down to the sea edge again and soon put many miles behind us. We pass Cannington and Combwich. It is very pretty around here. The drizzle comes, unfortunately, and then real rain. We pass a little school in Stogursey when we meet The Rev. Peter Pengelley. He chats to us for a few minutes and then takes us into the school to shelter.

Of course George gets introduced to the Headmaster, Mr. Knight, and then the inevitable happens. Once more George gives his talk, the children play with me, George gets his cup of coffee, the first hot drink for two days he says, and then we are on our way again.

Out of the village.we pass Kilve and then drop down a very steep hill into Watchet. It is here that George sees The Milk Bar cafe, and he reckons a cup of tea would go down a treat. George gets three large cups of tea, then the ladies behind the counter say they are having a party for all their customers as they are closing down. George said it was quite sad, as he has been made so welcome, and when we did set off we received a rousing cheer from all the good people.

Feeling much refreshed we set off towards the village of Blue Anchor. George notes the broken sea wall as we walk along the front. He says the seas must be really rough around here.

We pass through Dunster with its castle high on the hill. We call on George's Aunt, who he is very pleased to see. The first member of the family he has seen for eight and a half months. George and I spend the night in conversation before a nice warm fire, then its a bath and bed for George, while I am happy to remain in front of the fire.

George gets up about 8 am. Aunty and I are already about, and we have been outside for a little walk. George said he had a lovely night. He reads his mail which is waiting for him, and writes a couple of letters back. We phone Mum, and then after dinner George and I go for another short walk. We end up in the woods, and bring back an armful of firewood for Aunty. This day, George says is for relaxation, in a warm home in beautiful countryside.

CHAPTER 21

Dunster to Newquay

Another day to relax in. After breakfast George and I go for a walk and come back with a load of firewood again. I run among the trees and really enjoy scuffing around in the dead leaves. George says we must continue our journey to-morrow, so to make the most of to-day.

We awake to the 14th of November and we are up to day 259. We must say goodbye to Aunty, and George and I give her lots of kisses. We make our way again towards the Devon border. First however we must go through Minehead, and George says to me we will find it hard from now on as the last three days have been so perfect. The winds are fierce this morning and icy cold. George says he has left my chain behind at Dunster, so we will have to get another one. I tell him not to bother, but on passing a pet shop we go in and make the purchase. We make our way to the news office, more pictures and story telling. I am fed up and go to sleep in the corner, while George enjoys a hot coffee. We then start off on what is called The Neptune coastal path, which George says will take us to the end of our journey. I looked around carefully, but I didn't see Neptune anywhere.

We climb up a very steep hill and eventually arrive on the top of Exmoor. I must be very careful and keep near George as there is a steep cliff on my right which drops right away to the waves below. We now follow miles of coastal path, all clearly marked for a change, until we see Porlock in the distance. We soon pass Porlock Weir and head on for Lynmouth. We are at last in Devon, George says. I suggest we nip home across the county quick. No-one would know, but

George says we have to go around Cornwall yet, we must not cheat on the last leg. The shelter situation is non-existent, so we have to find a wind shielded spot for the tent to go up.

When we find a forest we stop although it is only 3.45 pm. It is very cold, and I think of the warm fire of last night. We were both cold in the night, so George allowed me to cuddle up, I even managed to get into the sleeping bag for a little way. We awoke the next morning to a hard frost. We pack up quickly and get going to wake up our circulation. George gets out his old R.A.F. gloves. This is the first time he has ever worn them on the walk, he says his fingers are all numb from taking down the tent. The only problem apart from the cold, he says, is the lack of human contact. He feels so lonely, there is not a soul in sight. I'm not surprised, I answer, its only fools like us who are walking the cliffs in late November.

We pass Martinhoe. George realizes his water bottle is nearly empty. We stop at a cottage to ask for a refill, and meet Major and Mrs Jordan. We are asked in, given lovely hot drinks and offered a bed for the night. I quickly accept for George before he can say anything. I find the fire and stretch out before it, without an invitation. George is very happy. A good roof, a good bed and good company all round. "People are kind wherever they live", George says.

After a good breakfast the next morning we set off again through Devon. We wave our goodbyes and Thanks, and then its off into the mist. We pass through Combe Martin where we once again stock up. I get some biscuits from a shop keeper, and then we soon cover the five mile stretch into Ilfracombe. We pass a field when we are surprised to be observed by some funny things with long necks. I have never seen anything like it. I was going to bark, but I realized

they didn't have any horns, so I didn't bother.
George said they were Llamas. He said they usually
live abroad and didn't know what they were doing here.
On enquiring however, from a gentleman passing by, it
was explained that they live in the wildpark which was
nearby. George and he shake hands and we all go our
separate ways.

We pass through Ilfracombe and set out up the long
hill, when we are invited by a Mr. amd Mrs. White to
come into their home for a cup of tea, before we
finally make it to the top. This was very nice, and
then George says we must start to find our shelter for
the night. We see a sign for Mortehoe just before
Woolacombe. The water side is absolutely deserted,
the only sound we hear is the church clock in Mortehoe
chiming four. George writes up his notes, and then we
walk to Woolacombe, where we see a shed across an open
park. It is open one end, but George says we can make
ourselves comfortable. He says he can see the outline
of Lundy Island across the water. Me, I can only see
sheep jumping over a gate.

The sky is overcast the next morning, but we pack up
quickly, and then we start to walk the golden sands
from Woolacombe to Pickwell and Croyde Bay. We pass
through the busy little town of Braunton towards
Barnstaple, and so down the other side of the river
towards Instow and Bideford. A police car pulls up
and advises George to put me on a lead, as the
motorists are crazy in this part of the world. They
are crazy everywhere if you ask me, but George does as
he is bid, and I feel miserable. Still never mind,
there must be some more lanes ahead, somewhere.

We purchase supplies, and I manage to get a bone from
a friendly butcher. We pass through Bickington and
Fremington on our way to Bideford. George says it is
beginning to get dimpsy, although it is only 3.30 pm,

and we will have to think about our shelter for tonight. At Yelland, George spots a shed across a few fields, so we go to investigate. We cross a field of sheep, and I stay close to George, I really am too tired to bother with a round-up. I nearly step on a pheasant, who screeches and flies off to a thicket, and then we look in the shed. It has a loft and several bales of hay, so George lifts me up to the loft, throws up his kit, and then we make ourselves comfy for the night.

We hear several low flying air craft from nearby Chivenor, which we passed earlier, but nothing keeps us awake, and we settle in early for a good sleep.

We awake after a good warm sleep and make ready for our start to Bideford. We are advised by a nice farmer to follow the railway line as it will be much quieter than the road. We are happy to do this, especially as there are no trains. We soon arrive in Bideford. We cross over the long road bridge of many arches and then head out of the town for Westward Ho! We meet up with a young lady doing a survey of sorts. She makes a fuss of me, and she and George walk about a mile together before they have to split up. George says he was very glad of the company, although it was only for a short while.

We head on for Clovelly and then turn for Hartland, soon covering the three miles into the village. We meet the local vicar and a roadsweeper. I meet the local butcher and manage to weedle a bone out of him. George spots a cafe where we have a quick cup of tea, and then its on towards Stoke and the coast. Another shed comes into view. "That's our place for tonight" George says.

The next day seems to be a lot colder, and the forecast on the little radio says its going to get

colder. I give myself a quick shake, and make sure
that my winter coat is still growing well, and then we
head off down the lanes towards Stoke. The sea dashes
on the rocks below, and I keep well away from the
edge. We drop down through a forest, where I chase a
squirrel who then climbs up a tree. The track gets
pretty muddy, we cross over a a little stone bridge at
the bottom, and we then find ourselves in Cornwall.

The next point of call is Woodford and Coombe, as we
step out towards Bude. George stops for a mug of
coffee in Bude and then we climb up the hill the three
miles into Widemouth Bay.

We have walked quite a few miles to-day, when George
stops to talk to an old lady outside of her cottage.
She directs us to a shed where we can sleep the night.
However George has to hack his way in through
brambles, but once inside we are quite comfy. The
stars are out and all is right with our world.

We make an early morning start the next day, the air
is crisp and just right for walking. George is trying
to get more miles in per day now as the winter is
really upon us, and we both want to be home for
Christmas. George stops for his pot of tea in a
little cafe in Tintagel. We are the only customers,
and the lady serving tells George her life history in
about half an hour. George says he feels better and
warmed up again so after phoning home from a box in
the village, we start our walk again.

We pass many pretty cottages, and George has a chat
here and there with people working in their gardens.
I go up one or two paths, and look invitingly at the
warm insides, but no luck this time, although I get a
fuss made of me.

We drop down a woody valley into Trebetherick, we cross a stream and climb the hill the other side when George sees an old Quarry with a shed. He checks the shed and it is just the right size for both of us. We go in and shut the door. It is very cosy. Another day over as we settle for the night.

The forecast is for strong north winds, and boy, it was right. George gets out his old R.A.F. gloves, and I ruffle up my fur. We start out at 6 am and walk briskly to warm ourselves up.

We soon make it into Port Isaac, when we meet up with the local butcher. He was unloading his van, and the smell was delicious. He made a fuss of me and I get a bone, and then its on up the hill and out of the village, soon arriving at Portquin. We pass through many villages on this coast, but now we are really hurrying and hope to make Newquay before the night is upon us.

We arrive at Rock, where we are able to get a little ferryboat over to Padstow. I get carried again, and I was glad to get to the other side as the little boat rocked a lot in the choppy sea. We have saved about twelve miles George says by taking that little ferry, I did mumble that I wouldn't have minded walking the twelve miles, but we are over now so we head out for Bedruthan Steps.

We stop in St. Merryn George has a few words with three men who are renting a cottage to get away from the rat race in London for a few days. We are invited in for a cup of tea. George chats for so long that when we come out it is dark. We find a barn, it is freezing cold, so George gets into his sleeping bag with all his clothes on, we cuddle in to each other and are soon fast asleep. So much for Newquay today!!

Next morning the world is white. The heavy frost of last night has not yet melted. We get going quickly, and George has a jumping up and down session to get things moving. My things are going O.K. so we pack up and step it out.

George stops to help a few ducks who are trying to swim on top of the ice on their pond. He throws in a few large bricks to break the ice of last night, and I presume the ducks are pleased after we have left. It is only just gone three o'clock, but George says we will start looking in the daylight as it looks like, and feels like, being another very cold night.

A spot of snow is falling when we see rather a nice barn. George says it looks very smart as though its in the process of being re-built. However there are a few bales of straw and it looks comfy, so we climb inside. We are up to day 267 and it is the 22nd of November. The time is 3.30pm.

CHAPTER 22

Newquay to Falmouth.

We wake up after a freezing night, to heavy frost on the ground. George says we will get going quickly and try and make Portreath today as he can then meet up with Graham and Sally May at their home. He puts on his thermal gear this morning for the first time. It's still dark, but George packs up and we get going to try and warm ourselves up. We look out over the sea at Perranporth to a calm water, not many waves this morning. No wind hardly, which is a blessing. I spot two donkeys hanging their heads over a gate. I go over and have a quick word with them, and they agree it has been a jolly cold night. We touch noses, they are so friendly.

On again towards St. Agnes. George chats to a friendly farmer on the way who is milking his cows in the milking parlour, the buzz of the machinery floats on the still air. We stop again to chat to some men felling a big tree, the menfolk all share a big mug of coffee, including George, then we stock up with a few provisions in the next village, and soon we arrive on the outskirts of Portreath.

We get directions to Sally and Graham's home, which we soon find and get a good reception. I meet their little daughter, Flair, and the grandparents. Oh it is lovely to be in a house again. George has a bath, much needed I may add, and a shave. Then after tea he and Graham go down to the local for a quick one, while I stay at home and keep Sally and Flair company. They arrive back before long and then its to bed in a nice warm house. No cuddling up to-night to try and keep the frost out. Tony, my friend of many weeks back comes with his wife Judith to meet us, he sleeps over for the night, and is going to walk a little way with us again tomorrow.

Tony and George get woken up with a mug of coffee in the morning. They both, as well as me, get a good breakfast, and then we thank Graham and Sally for their kindness and we are all off once again. George is very happy this morning because of Tony's company.

We head out of the village along the coastal path and observe the still calm sea. There is a light wind, but not the bitter wind of a couple of days back. There is a mist out over the channel. Minty (Tony's dog), and I scurry ahead of the men, I am pleased for her company too, and we really get on well together. The last time we walked together was around Anglesey. At St. Ives Bay, we are able to walk along the beach for a bit, it is really good, and Minty and I chase about the sands like a couple of young things. It is absolutely deserted, and stays like that until we arrive in Hayle

We go into the town and George and Tony purchase two real Cornish pasties, from the Pendarnes arms. George then buys a third one which Minty and I have between us. They have half a pint of ale each and then we say goodbye to our very jovial landlord and make our way towards St. Ives. Here we all meet up with Judith again, who drives us back in her car to their cottage for the night. On the way we call into Penzance newspaper offices to give our account to date.

It is nice to have another warm night with a roof over our heads. We awake at 7 am with a cup of tea brought to us by Tony. We did call at Tony's local last night, and both the men say they have thick heads this morning. Serves them right I thought, however they said it was worth it.

There is drizzle about this morning, but it helps the head situation. Judith drives us over to St. Ives and drops us all off where she picked us up yesterday. We all set off once again, with Minty and I leading the way. We climb up a long hill and start on the thirteen miles to St. Just. So far our walk is very enjoyable. No-one about, George and Tony wake up all the birds with their chatter. No traffic and Minty and I are just content to be together.

The scenery is rugged, with great pieces of granite rock sticking up here and there, through the mist on our left. The rain now comes on quite hard, so George and Tony stop for a pint and a meal at The Gurnard's Head Hotel. There is a big sign which says NO DOGS, so Minty and I have to wait in the front porch.

Suddenly there is an awful racket, a man starts shouting and swearing at us. It wakes up both Minty and myself. He bashes on the window to George, and then goes into the pub. Minty and I are both alarmed as we have done nothing wrong. The man continues to shout at George and Tony, and so much abuse is going on that both the men cancel their meal, drink up their ale, and leave the man, his dreadful manners, and the pub. George said to me that he could no longer tolerate the man's bad manners, and it is the first unkindness we have been shown since the man in Scotland refused us water, all that way back.

We continue our walk westward, passing several old tin mines along the way, we hear the sound of distant fog horns from the various lighthouses along the coast. The rain still rains, and the winds have now risen to gale force. Not so enjoyable a walk as when we first set out. Tony is having a bit of trouble with his left foot, and we all walk slower. We stop off at a local store at Botallack, and meet the people who run it. They seem very nice and give George a copy of yesterdays newspaper. They were very sorry about the aggravation at the last hotel. Another warm bed for to-night, lovely I thought, but nearly home Judith has a slight argument with a land rover type. We are all O.K. but the front wing has a nasty dent.

We arrive back to a lovely warm house, a hot bath, gallons of tea and a good meal. Judith and Tony have a night out while George and I and Minty look after the two little girls.

The next morning we are away at eight am. Judith takes us by car to the spot she picked us up at yesterday, and we carry on with our walk. This idea is fabulous, I hope it happens all the way home. But George says it is just lucky we are going around in a circle as it were.

We reach Lands End at 11.45am. It is raining hard so we cant see much; however we hear the waves crashing on the rocks below. We beat a hasty retreat and head for The Logan Rock. We call into the Logan Rock public house, and get a very warm welcome, really hot Cornish Pasties, which taste especially good.

George and Tony chat to the locals, while Minty and I stretch out in front of the warm fire. We set off once again to walk the four miles to Lamorna. Judith now arrives to take us back once more to the cottage. We have at last rounded the corner bringing to an end our five month long walk south after Cape Wrath in Scotland. We will now start the last stretch tomorrow and head for Exeter. George hopes at this stage to be home by the 17th of December, but he says it is difficult to predict exactly. But for now we return to a nice meal, with perhaps a couple of pints of ale at Penzance.

Spots of rain on the window next morning announce another wet day. Judith takes both Tony and George and my friend and I back to Lamorna, where we were picked up last night. We take a pretty and enjoyable lane to Mousehole. The rain actually stops, but there is a stiff breeze blowing in off the sea. We look right out over Mounts Bay and can just see the other side to Cudden Point through the gently rising mist.

George finds Tony's company most rewarding, although Tony finds his foot problem is still with us, so our progress is a little slow. I love to have Minty with me, and we have a good chatter in our doggy way about different things. We proceed along the waterfront and soon arrive at Newlyn, stopping briefly to observe the harbour wall and the huge waves which come periodically and bash over it. We all watch several surfers in the rough seas, and how they seem to be enjoying themselves despite the cold weather.

We pass through the little town and head off towards Penzance. The clouds of this morning seem to have cleared and we see an area of blue sky and for a little while the sun shines. We walk on the sands for a short distance until we come to a gulley too wide to jump across with water pouring out to sea. Minty and I swim across and enjoy ourselves, while George and Tony have to return to a bridge to cross over. The tide is going out which reveals a long stone causeway out to St. Michael's Mount. We take a slight detour out to the Mount, but both Minty and I are a little wary of the surrounding water which slushes up every now and again.

Returning to the mainland we all find our way to The Mexican Arms, public house, where George and Tony have a good lunch and good conversation from a friendly landlord, before we set out again from Marazion to cover the few miles to Goldsithney. Our arranged picking up spot for Judith. Once more a lovely warm bed at Catchall, a hot bath and a couple of drinks at The Logan Rock. Oh, long may this continue.

Tony brings in the usual cup of tea, and then we get ready again for the day ahead. To-day however, we are going to rest, so a lovely dozy day by the fire will do me I say. However, George says he must go into Penzance to report to the news office. He is taken by car, and then we all get ready for the christening of Judiths and Tony's two daughters at Sancreed Church. The rest of the family arrive from Exeter and after lunch we all drive out to the Church for a quiet and personal ceremony, which was simple, yet splendid. We later return to the house for yet more good food. Minty and I were very good, and watched everything from the church porch.

The family finally dispersed home towards Devonshire. I looked longingly at the car and wondered whether I could be a stow-away, but I expect George would miss my company, he said I was important to him. Tony and George have a final few beers at the local pub. They meet Mrs Smith the wife of a lighthouse keeper, who George says was fantastic, with the same humour as he and Tony. Home to bed and a lovely sleep.

Next day we are returned to our pick-up point, and Judith goes off shopping in Helston. The four of us trudge on, although not raining the morning is damp. We head towards Porthleven, and drop down to the harbour. There are many small boats bobbing around at anchor. Minty and I see a large black cat and we give chase until he jumps through a thicket of brambles. I am not going to get pricked for a silly old cat. We head on towards Helston, with only about two miles to go when Judith arrives to pick up Tony and Minty. They are parting with us now, and George and I feel very miserable. It has been lovely having them with us these past few days, but we are getting farther and farther from the house, and we can no longer return to our lovely warm bed.

With much sorrow we wave goodbye, we thank Judith for all our nights sleep at the cottage, and the meals, and then, turning a corner they are out of sight. George and I feel very low, he puts me on a lead for a little while, in case I decide to find my way back to Minty, and then we enter Helston and find some provisions to carry on with. We find the local news office where we meet Noel Perry, who makes George a cup of coffee. We give our story with photos and then we get directions to the Martin family's home, where George has a letter to deliver. It was given to him in Dumfries in Scotland, on the 31st of August.

We hand over the letter to John and Katie Martin outside their home. We are invited in, given a lovely meal and a bed for the night, so once more we have a roof which we are very glad of as it is raining outside. We are awakened by John at 6.30 am, and have a big cooked breakfast, which George says will really set him up for the day. George checks the weather, and we find that there is a thick, damp mist everywhere. I also have a good breakfast, and then we have to say goodbye to John and Katie and their small son Kevin, for looking after us so well last night.

It is the last day of November to-day and we are up to day 275. Off again on our travels, on the busy main road out of Helston. We head towards Mullion and pass the busy navy base at Culdrose. Our vision is no more than fifty yards and I keep close to George. There are several birds sitting on the telegraph wires, I don't suppose they can see where to fly. I look at some sheep sitting in the field, we speak to a farmer who they belong to. He makes a fuss of me and then

after chatting with George for a while, we are invited
into the farmhouse for a mug of tea.

Mrs Freeman, the farmers wife gives George a piece of
her homemade cake, actually I think he ate the lot. I
sit in front of a lovely fire, while Farmer Freeman
and George chat on for about an hour. Then we have to
leave our friends behind as we trudge on towards
Mullion, and then the Point at the Lizard. We know
better than to look for a place near the lighthouse at
the end to spend the night, especially with the heavy
mist still about. We make it to Ruan Minor, and then
through the quiet sleepy little villages to Coverack.
There doesn't seem any sheds or barns around, so
George puts up the tent on a bit of grass and we
settle for the night.

Next morning is a great improvement on the weather.
The wind came up in the night, and blew the mists
away, however it made taking down the tent a bit of a
job, and I got tangled up with it once or twice, I was
only trying to help I said to George, but he told me
to keep out of the way.

To-day is the 1st of December, it feels like it too.
We set out at a brisk pace as the sun is actually
shining for a while. George then discovers he has
lost his hat. We retrace our steps for a mile to our
campsite, but no hat. George continues to walk
onwards saying he will have to buy another because his
ears are cold, when we meet up with a Mr. Elliott, out
walking his red setter. He is interested in our
story, and has read bits about us in the newspaper
when we are invited back to his house for a cup of
tea. George says his tent feels uncomfortable the way
it was packed, so he re-packs it at Mr. Elliotts, and
also finds his hat, so he is complete once more. Mr.
Elliotts cup of tea turns out to be another fantastic
breakfast. He contacts the local school, and once

more we are invited to speak to the children. We get many questions and lots of interest and then its on again. Mr. Elliott joins us for a mile out of the town when we meet up with the local vicar, with whom we all shake hands, and we also say goodbye to Mr. Elliott as he returns to the village, with the vicar.

George and I set off at a good fast pace, as George wants to reach Falmouth this evening, and call on Mr. and Mrs. Dalton who live there. We plod on through the now bare countryside, eventually crossing the Helford river and heading on towards Rosemullion Head. The last signpost for Falmouth said seven miles, and the darkness is falling. As we walk on George gets out his torch to let cars and other people know we are about. I do not like this night walking at all, there are all sorts of sounds that I cannot make out.

We find the right address in Falmouth without too much trouble. We, again, are given a good welcome. I was in first this time, I know where to find the fires now. George and I were given a good feed, a hot bath and a warm bed. So all is right with the world.

We awoke at 8.30am, after a very restful night. After breakfast, Mr. Dalton contacts the local radio station, and we do a live broadcast which goes out at Mid-day. George and I then have a walk around the town, I manage to get a couple of bones given me, and then we return to the house for just one more night. Next day after another good breakfast, George and I are taken down to the ferry to check the times of departure for St. Mawes. Apparently they do not run on a Sunday, as far as I was concerned they need not run at all. Anyway, all in all we were invited to stay yet another night at the house. This was extremely kind of them, and we spent the rest of the day just lazing around. Not only that but Mrs Dalton has rung the harbour master at Mevagissey, a

Mr.Rafferty, to arrange a stopping off place for us tomorrow night. She said it was much too cold to sleep outside, this weather. I heartily agree with her, so tomorrow we have something nice to look forward to. George says with a bit of luck we will be able to get a roof over our heads until Plymouth.

Next day we spent another restful day, it is now the 4th of December, and to-day, at the Norway Inn, we meet Mrs Angela Herbert,(the round the world yachtswoman).

Tomorrow we must continue our walk after our lovely rest of the past few days.

CHAPTER 23

Falmouth to Exminster

The forecast for to-day is sunshine, so George and I make an early start. We thank Mr and Mrs Dalton for all their kindness, and with a good breakfast inside both of us we set out on the last part of our journey.

Mr and Mrs Dalton come down to the ferry to see us off, which was very nice of them. We thank them again for the last four days. I, by the way, offered to stay, especially with the ferry coming in, but George said not to be a baby, and I got carried on again. We both wave goodbye as we head across the bay.

Once more, on land, which is nice and hard under my feet, we set off again and head towards Portscatho. We follow a quiet road for several miles when a car pulls up. A nice couple have heard our broadcast, and seen us on television. They just wanted to wish us well for the rest of our journey. We walk on the beach for quite a while until we are in view of Portloe, then we follow the coastal path again for the next few miles. The view from the path is very nice, the sea is calm and the sun shines. George does have a moan about the hills going up and down though.

We soon pass through Portholland, and we follow the signs for Portmellon. We pass through an area of sheep, all of them with autumn lambs. George is very pleased that I stay by his side. We pass a man who is painting his gate. He and George have quite a chat. He then gives us directions to Mevagissey, and soon arrive in the town. George gets a few supplies and directions to the harbourmasters office and we meet Mr. Jim Rafferty. He takes George and I to his home, and I meet Tiger, a little friendly terrier, whom I

get on well with. He doesn't attack me once, so I
don't know where he got his name.

George has cups of tea and me a cold drink, and then
Mr Rafferty returns to his office for a while. I
flake out in front of the fire, and George catches up
on his postcard writing. Later, the family all return,
and another nice evening is spent among friends in a
lovely warm home. Mr Rafferty and George talk until
the early hours, while Tiger invites me to have a
little kip in his basket, which was very nice of him.

Next morning after a jolly good breakfast we have to
say goodbye to the family. Mr. Rafferty walks with me
a few miles, and then he returns to the harbour after
he and George shake hands, and with shouts of good
wishes to each other, we head out of the town for
Pentewan, then its Charlestown and Par. The road is
quiet so we once again make good progress. We arrive
at Fowey, when we come to another of those ferry
things, however the other side does not seem too far
away, so George manages to get me to walk on to this
one. We look for the signs for Looe and Polperro.
However we seem to get a bit lost. George meets a
nice couple who tell us we are four miles adrift. We
retrace our steps smartly and at last get on the right
road. We hope to make Looe before darkness falls so
we really have to hurry. The dusk begins to fall, and
the cars have started to put their headlights on, but
arriving at Looe we manage to find the home of Mr and
Mrs Joliff. We get a nice reception, welcome cups of
tea, a nice fire and a good meal and bed.

George says the night passes too quickly, I am
awakened by the noise of the seagulls out over the
quay. We get another good cooked breakfast, with
masses of tea, before we have to take our leave from
Mr. and Mrs Joliff. We wave our goodbyes and many

thanks and we turn our noses homeward again. George says it wont be long now before we are home.

We hope to get through Plymouth to-day. We arrive at Seaton beach, I have a bit of pain in my back leg, but manage to keep going, although I dont enjoy chasing about on the sand this time. George has a look at me, and then after a rest we get going again. The traffic is crazy George says, and puts me on the lead until we reach Saltash.

George now looks for the home of an old friend, Diana Acland. He gets directions and knocks on the door. A good welcome once again, while I find the fire. Pots of tea for George, a good hot bath, a shave, a meal and a warm bed, what more could a man want. I am content with just the fire and a bit of supper.

We are awoken by Anthony and William, Diana's two sons. I have a rough and tumble with them, and then after another good breakfast George and I are away to cross the road bridge into Plymouth and Devon. This by the way is only a brief detour as we are not starting properly until tomorrow morning, having been invited to spend another night with Diana. We are just making a visit to the newspaper offices to-day.

We get a good reception in the press offices. George gets a cup of coffee and I share someone's sandwiches. We then call on the local T.V. people, and will call on them again in the morning to do a recording. We now return to Saltash via the local radio station, to do an actual recording there and then. We are glad to return to Diana's as the rain is now very hard, and we shall be out of it before another night is over.

We return to Plymouth in the pouring rain next day, to do our 'Bit' at the T.V. studio. We find the film crew are out and we are asked to wait two hours for

them until midday. I go to sleep and George reads
anything he can find. At last a phone call comes
through to say they are sorry but they will have to
cancel our talk, as they won't be able to get back.

George is really fed up about this, as he stayed in
Plymouth an extra day to do this film, and now we are
over two hours late on our to-days walk. George is
not happy and after a phone call to Diana we both
return to her home for another warm night. Diana says
we have got a good mention in the newspaper with
pictures, so after a meal, George feels better for a
while, until we hear the news on the television, which
gives snow for tomorrow in certain parts of Devon.

We set off early the next day. This is the last week
for walking, George says, as he hopes to reach Exeter
by next Saturday. We leave our warm house once again,
and also Saltash as we have trudged right through the
centre of Plymouth to the other side. I run up and
down the road in front of George, with my ears pricked
up, my leg seems better and I know I am at last
homeward bound. My breath comes out like smoke in the
cold air, and on looking around I find that George's
is the same.

We pass through Newton Ferrers and Noss Mayo. Not
many people about. The sun is already going down over
Bigbury Bay when we decide we must find a place for
to-night. George sees an old summer house, in what
seems to be derelict gardens. We find some old
newspapers, and no signs of recent occupation, so we
will rest here for to-night. We both slept well but
were awakened by heavy rain on the summerhouse roof.
The forecast on George's radio, still says snow, so we
must hurry along.

At Holbeton village George rings his brother Bill, and
we arrange to meet up at Teignmouth. He also rings

Steve Phillips, who George and I stayed with way back at the start of this walk. I am very much looking forward to seeing them again as it is now over nine and a half months since we last met. We follow the signs for Aveton Gifford, and luckily for us the tide is out and we are able to walk along the tidal road, and head on towards Kingsbridge. The time is 3.30pm and night is coming on. George spots a shed and we check it out. This will do fine for tonight, and we are soon inside, and under cover, with again a roof over our heads. I find a nice bale of hay to snuggle into and soon we are both out for the count.

Next morning we awake to rain. It is day 287 and the 12th of December. After we have packed up the rain seems to have stopped for a while so we get going while we can. There is mud everywhere owing to last nights rain, but I suppose it could have been worse, it could be snowing this morning. Suddenly the pathway ends, and the only person about is a scarecrow, and he looks as though he has seen better days. George carries on and slides in the mud and lands on his bottom. We alter our direction and end up in a great big muddy pool. Eventually we find a muddy track of sorts, but goodness knows where we are.

We find a road and soon we walk into Kingsbridge, find the newspaper offices and do the necessary. We buy supplies and then we are observed by seven ducks, who have mistaken the road, presumably for their pond. Everywhere is so wet. The sun comes out as we leave the town. We do a quick diversion to Start Point and then up to Torcross and see the sign for Dartmouth.

We cross the sea front at Slapton Sands, the sea is very rough but we are away from it a little. We meet a lady who is taking out a pack of King Charles Spaniels. They all come over to me at once and while George chats away, I am surrounded. I don't like it one bit, and show my teeth at them all, keeping my tail firmly tucked between my legs. George says goodbye quickly and we soon walk away.

On reaching Kingswear we climb up over the hill towards Brixham. The sky is getting darker and just before Brixham we get a short sharp shower. We top up our supplies in the town, and then as it is 3.30pm we look for a place for the night. George spots an old shed in the garden of a ruined house, it is fine, and we are soon in and settled, just as the rain comes on again. George finds some old springs and he makes up a bed of sorts. I look askance at him and wonder whether he will last the night on such a contraption.

George said in the morning he would have been better off on the floor with me as the springs stuck in everywhere in the night, but he was too tired to move. I did try once to get in with George and stuck my cold nose against his skin, but he shouted and I returned to the floor. Golly we have been really spoiled with our wonderful nights when we had a real bed.

We arise at 7am as George says he would like to reach Jill Proffit to-day. A contact at Teignmouth. We set off along the busy road heading for Paignton and Torquay. I give chase to a school bus for quite away. George likes to see me run but he says it is dangerous, and I am not to do it. He says Mum would not be pleased if he arrived home without me. I stay obediently by his side.

The forecast for to-day was rain and high winds, but it is still dry at the moment, so we try and make good headway. We report to the newspaper office at Paignton, and as we walk the sea front, a photographer catches us up and we oblige him with some photos.

Along the sea front at Tor Bay the sea is really wild, rushing in against the sea wall with such a thump. It really frightens me and I am glad when we move away. George now seeks Warren road, where a freelance news agency that contacted George when he was at Plymouth, are established. We get a good reception and George has a hot drink, the first he has had for four days, and through all this cold weather he was badly in need of this. Photos again and then we follow the coast road to Shaldon.

We see the waves dashing up the Thatcher rock, and George hangs on to his woolly hat as the winds blow even stronger. Soon we arrive at the top of the hill above Shaldon, and we then drop down into the village.

We get directions from a lollipop lady as to the whereabouts of Cliff road, George and I cross over Shaldon Bridge and turn into the town of Teignmouth. We find the home of Jill, but find she is out. However she has left us a note to say she will return soon and she has left a thermos of hot drink by the front door. This is very welcome says George, and even I get some, when it has cooled.

The rain comes harder and soon Jill and her husband Ray arrive home. We are both made very welcome and George gets a hot bath and a hot meal, which does him the world of good. Me, I find a lovely fire, and sprawl out in front of it. There are already four dogs in the house, but they all make me welcome, and leave me the best place in front of the fire. George says it is lovely to be civilized again.

George has arranged to meet the press people to-day, so more photos etc. The phone rings continuously as more and more press people are interested in us, and the T.V. people, just because we are nearing home and have done it.

I don't think that half of them ever thought we would. When they ring up, each department has told us not to let anyone else in on the story. By the end of the day both George and Jill have headaches. We then hear that the local T.V. don't think they can make it for our return. George says this is ironic as all the other T.V. companies throughout G.Britain, have welcomed us with open arms. Yet to our own district of Devon we are unimportant.

We meet up with brother Bill and Steve this evening, George said it was good to see them. He arranges to meet Steve at Exminster tomorrow. But now it is another good sleep, at last the winds have stopped for a while. I hope it lasts a few days.

The next day, number 291 is the 16th. of December. We get up quickly and the phone starts ringing. We can see from the kitchen window that the sea is still rough, the winds are also about and make all the trees sway. After a good breakfast we make our way towards Dawlish and Exminster. Jill and Ray and three of the four dogs walk part of the way with us, before we have to say goodbye, and thank you for two nights of luxury and kindness.

We reach Dawlish and attempt to walk along the seafront, but the tide is in and huge waves are breaking over the top, so we stick to the road, and while walking on this Exeter road we hear a voice call to George. It is Marion Bartle, an old nursing friend of George's, As George has not seen her for over a year, he tells her our story. She says she'll try and be in Exeter for our return tomorrow. We're on the Dawlish Warren road when we're stopped by a policeman. He requires some identification from George. George thinks this is quite funny, as we have completed nearly 7,000 miles, and it's the first time the police have stopped us. He seems a reasonable chap and asks for George's driving licence, as he didn't seem to believe George's story. I had to sit on my haunches and laugh. We didn't even have a car, leave alone a licence. I licked his hand and he seemed to like it. I got a pat and then he said to carry on. Whether he still didn't believe us I don't know, but we carried on over the harbour bridge to Starcross.

We follow the road to Powderham when the rain comes on again. We see the castle on our left between the trees. As we reach Exminster village, darkness comes down. Another day is passed, but tomorrow we will be home. We press on as it is now 5pm, when eventually we meet Steve by the Big Motel which overlooks the lights of Exeter. We have a roof again tonight, as Steve is taking us home to Newton Poppleford, and will return us to this spot tomorrow. Marie gives us a good welcome, and then its a bath, a shave, delicious food and then bed. Tomorrow we see Mum.

CHAPTER 55

HOMEWARD BOUND

We are up to day 292 and it is the 17th of December. We are awoken by Steve and Marie's little girl, as we were when we were on day two of our walk. She sings to me Twinkle, twinkle little star. I join in, but George tells me to shut up and listen.

After breakfast, Steve takes George and I back to the spot he picked us up from yesterday. As he drives off two sets of pressmen approach, wanting exclusive rights to our story. A slight argument takes place, and George and I keep out of the way. We start off to finish our journey in haste, but a car picks us up and takes us back to Powderham castle, where they want photographs taken. The car behind follows at speed, but we then eventually manage to shake them off.

We are returned to the Motel to complete our walk into Exeter. We walk through the crowded streets of all the Christmas shoppers, and make our way to the local newspaper offices, where, owing to the fact that we are late, our reception was limited to just two people. Our cousin Lisa and Sister-in-Law Sue. It was a tremendous feeling to greet them both, and I know they have been waiting for us since 10 am. and it is now 2 pm. George says he fully appreciates them staying on, and while cousin Lisa catches the bus home, Sue says she will walk with me to Topsham.

The rain comes on quite heavy but we don't mind, it is lovely to meet up with family again.

The miles soon pass and George calls on a few old friends on the way home, including Mike Chanter who saw George and I start on this journey so long ago.

We get a wonderful welcome home, including Jill and Ray, and we have a houseful of friends. There are many photographs taken and celebrations. We then go to The New Inn at Broadclyst, and a tremendous reunion follows. George says its good to see everybody again, and to be home. I thoroughly agree and tell everyone so.

George says he has completed a four year dream being able to complete this walk, and has certainly made him appreciate the good things in life. This is, Good Health which makes one the richest person in the world. He appreciates many things since this walk, that before he took for granted. A warm home, good HOT food, friends etc., so many good things that he never noticed before. He said the newspapers and T.V. seem to be destroying peoples ability to be happy and content, all the doom and gloom that we get in the daily news sells papers, when in Georges's opinions life in Britain isn't really so bad, if we only open our eyes and see all the beauty around us.

During this walk George and I made about 200 friends, and only met three people who weren't very nice, and of those three George has known worse. So all in all the story that George would like to promote is all the good things for a change, if only we open our eyes to see them.

On the 18th of December, George and I spend a quiet day at home, prior to going to London tomorrow, where we have to do an interview on B.B.C. Television for the Blue Peter show. George says this will be a tremendous experience, and I will meet Goldie, the programmes famous labrador. Goldie is sick on the floor, perhaps it was the excitement of meeting me. We all seem to do well, and George and I enjoyed it, being stars at last, this resulted in a donation from the B.B.C. to me of a huge bone.

We have a relaxed journey home by train, and we are met at St. David's by Jill, who takes us once more to The New Inn to account for our reactions to the T.V. show. It's then home to Topsham at 11.30pm. We are greeted by the news that George and I are to return to London the next day to do another show on T.V.

Two days later we are awoken by the postman dropping hundreds of cards in the hall from the letter box.

At 11 am we travel to The Blue Ball public house at Sidford, to a reception for us by The Animal Rescue Centre. All the dogs in care are brought to welcome me, and I just enjoy every minute of it. Photos are taken and then I am presented with The Spillers golden bone award, and we all enjoy a nice meal.

I have been told I have gone into The Animal Guiness Book of records, as the first dog to have walked 7,000 miles. At the moment if you come to our door I am having a well earned kip, its been going on for a week now, so please knock quietly.

OBITUARY.

It is with great sadness that we have to report the death of Jack at the grand old age of 17 years. (i.e. 119 human years).

Jack died on Saturday 16th of August 1997. at 7.30 p.m. at his home, from old age and the heat of the August sun, (just 6 weeks before the launch of this book). He died in his own bed with his own blanket and with George at his side.

He was buried on a common piece of land near to his home, leading up to Stoke Woods on the outskirts of Exeter, where you can look out over the fields for miles and see the sea beyond, it was here that he loved to walk and play with his friends.

A baby Oak tree has been planted on his grave.

If you ever walk near that place and hear a soft pad, pad, pad, behind you, and the rustle of dead leaves, don't worry, it is only Jack starting out on his long trek around the coastpath of Heaven.